ORTHO'S® All About

Flowering Trees & Shrubs

Written by Harrison L. Flint

Meredith® Books
Des Moines, Iowa

Ortho® Books
An imprint of Meredith® Books

All About Flowering Trees & Shrubs
Editor: Michael McKinley
Senior Associate Design Director: Tom Wegner
Assistant Editor: Harijs Priekulis
Copy Chief: Terri Fredrickson
Managers, Book Production: Pam Kvitne, Marjorie J. Schenkelberg
Contributing Copy Editor: Barbara Feller-Roth
ContributingTechnical Proofreader: Fran Gardner
Contributing Proofreaders: Beth Lastine, Ellie Sweeney
Contributing Illustrator: Mike Eagleton
Contributing Map Illustrator: Jana Fothergill
Indexer: Ellen Davenport
Electronic Production Coordinator: Paula Forest
Editorial and Design Assistants: Kathleen Stevens, Karen Schirm

Additional Editorial Contributions from Art Rep Services
Director: Chip Nadeau
Designers: Ik Design

Meredith® Books
Editor in Chief: James D. Blume
Design Director: Matt Strelecki
Managing Editor: Gregory H. Kayko
Executive Editor, Gardening and Home Improvement: Benjamin W. Allen

Director, Sales, Special Markets: Rita McMullen
Director, Sales, Premiums: Michael A. Peterson
Director, Sales, Retail: Tom Wierzbicki
Director, Book Marketing: Brad Elmitt
Director, Operations: George A. Susral
Director, Production: Douglas M. Johnston

Meredith Publishing Group
President, Publishing Group: Stephen M. Lacy

Meredith Corporation
Chairman and Chief Executive Officer: William T. Kerr

Chairman of the Executive Committee: E.T. Meredith III

Thanks to
Janet Anderson, Robin Cox, Mary Irene Swartz, Rosemary A. Kautzky, Spectrum Communication Services, Inc.

Photographers
(Photographers credited may retain copyright © to the listed photographs.)
L = Left, R = Right, C = Center, B = Bottom, T = Top
William D. Adams: 14BL, 24T, 38B, 83T; **Gay Bumgarner:** 82B; **Patricia J. Bruno/Positive Images:** 52B; **David Cavagnaro:** 8BR, 51TL, 51BR, 79TC; **Candace Cochrane/Positive Images:** 3T, 4; **Catriona Tudor Erler:** 8T, 11TL, 22L, 67BL, 85T; **Derek Fell:** 25B, 39C, 44T, 44B, 45T, 45BC, 45B, 46C, 48T, 50C, 52C, 53T, 54T, 57B, 58, 60C, 61T, 61B, 64B, 69B, 70T, 72B, 73TR, 74BL, 75TL, 75B, 80BL, 80BC, 80TR, 81CR, 85B, 88TR, 87R, 88B; **Harrison Flint:** 8BL, 38C, 41T, 47C, 63T, 70C, 78TL; **Susan M. Glascock:** 76BCL, 79BL; **John Glover:** 9T, 11TR, 17, 19TR, 57T, 59C, 65T, 66B, 72T; **John Glover/Garden Picture Library:** 42B, 78TR; **Anne Gordon:** 56TR, 88TC; **Jerry Harpur:** 39T; **Marcus Harpur:** 14BR, 65C; **Marijke Heuff/Garden Picture Library:** 49T; **Neil Holmes/Garden Picture Library:** 11B, 46T; **Saxon Holt:** 3TC, 3BC, 6B, 14T, 18TL, 22R, 24B, 27T, 36B, 47B, 49C, 54B, 68C, 74T, 81TL, 86T, 87L, 89T; **Bill Johnson:** 56TL, 56B, 67BR; **Rosemary Kautzky:** 37C; **Donna & Tom Krischan:** 86C; **Lamontagne/Garden Picture Library:** 51TR; **Andrew Lawson:** 7B, 41C, 60B, 87C, 87T, 88C, 90; **Lee Lockwood/Positive Images:** 84T; **Janet Loughrey:** 5BL, 5BR, 41B, 44C, 45TC, 48C, 53C, 55T, 68B, 73BR, 79T, 89C; **David McDonald/PhotoGarden:** 5T, 6T, 7T, 10T, 43B, 49B, 53B, 73L; **Michael McKinley:** 80TL, 81TC; **Ortho Library:** 28, 29, 30, 31, 32, 33; **Jerry Pavia:** 9B, 10B, 36T, 47T, 52T, 69C, 76T, 76BL, 81B, 81C, 83B; **Ben Phillips/Positive Images:** 35, 46, 63B; **Howard Rice/Garden Picture Library:** 40TL, 60T, 66T; **Richard Shiell:** 18TR, 36C, 38T, 42T, 42C, 51BL, 57TC, 59T, 61C, 62T, 62C, 64T, 71T, 77CL, 78BL, 79BR, 80BR, 81TR, 82T, 82C, 87B; **Pam Spaulding/Positive Images:** 19TL, 43T; **Betsy Strauch:** 78BC; **Joseph G. Strauch, Jr.:** 37B, 40B, 55C, 55Bi, 65B, 67T, 69T, 72C, 74BR, 76BL, 76BCR, 77T, 77BR, 78C, 78BR, 83C, 86B; **Studio Central:** 16B; **Michael S. Thompson:** 3B, 16T, 26, 27 BL, 27BR, 34L, 34R,, 37T, 43C, 48B, 50B, 55B, 57BC, 59B, 62B, 63C, 70B, 71B, 74BC, 75TR, 76C, 76BR, 76CR, 78TC, 81LC, 84C, 88L, 89B; **Rick Wetherbee:** 78CR; **Justyn Willsmore:** 25T, 39B, 40TR, 50T, 54C, 66C, 68T, 71C, 84B, 85C

On the cover: Japanese snowbell *(Styrax japonicum)* is a small tree that is especially lovely when placed arching over a pathway so that you can look up into its pendulous flowers. A red rhododendron appears even more brilliant against the snowy white flowers. Photograph by Michael S. Thompson.

All of us at Ortho® Books are dedicated to providing you with the information and ideas you need to enhance your home and garden. We welcome your comments and suggestions about this book. Write to us at:
Meredith Corporation
Ortho Gardening Books
1716 Locust St.
Des Moines, IA 50309–3023

If you would like to purchase any of our gardening, home improvement, cooking, crafts, or home decorating and design books, check wherever quality books are sold. Or visit us at: meredithbooks.com

If you would like more information on other Ortho products, call 800-225-2883 or visit us at: www.ortho.com

Library of Congress Control Number: 2001132248
ISBN: 0-897-21-480-3

Note to the Readers: Due to differing conditions, tools, and individual skills, Meredith Corporation assumes no responsibility for any damages, injuries suffered, or losses incurred as a result of following the information published in this book. Before beginning any project, review the instructions carefully, and if any doubts or questions remain, consult local experts or authorities. Because codes and regulations vary greatly, you always should check with authorities to ensure that your project complies with all applicable local codes and regulations. Always read and observe all of the safety precautions provided by manufacturers of any tools, equipment, or supplies, and follow all accepted safety procedures.

DESIGNING WITH COLOR

IN THIS SECTION

Mention beautiful gardens, and the first thing you think about is colorful flowers. Color stimulates the eye and refreshes the spirit. Would a garden photographed in black and white be as inspiring?

We appreciate colorful flowers wherever we see them: in alpine meadows in summer; in the Japanese cherry blossoms around the Tidal Basin in Washington, D.C., in April; or in a single flowering crabapple tree in a neighbor's yard in May. In fleeting moments it occurs to us that we could enjoy superb color in our own gardens. Perhaps we are intimidated in our own gardening when we see other gardens that realize the full potential of color. Remember that a colorful garden is a possibility for any gardener, but such a garden is not built in a day. It happens by starting with the basics, having a plan, and summoning up some patience. Then you can relax and proceed, knowing the process can be as rewarding as the result.

In a Midwestern garden, a canopy of pink flowering dogwood underplanted with Japanese kerria provides striking color contrast in late spring.

Flowering trees and shrubs are woody plants. Trees usually have single trunks and grow 20 feet tall or more; shrubs are shorter and have multiple stems rising from the ground. There are exceptions: Star magnolia *(Magnolia stellata)* is a tree, but seldom grows more than 15 feet tall and may have more than one trunk; Siebold viburnum *(Viburnum sieboldii)* and southern black haw *(Viburnum rufidulum)* have true shrub habits but can reach 25 to 30 feet and would be called trees if trained into tree form. Trees and shrubs together form the bones of the garden and can determine its principal color scheme. Nonwoody annual and perennial flowering plants can be added later to reinforce or complement the colors of the woody plants and give your garden a finished look.

Before you select trees and shrubs for their flowering effect, consider their size, hardiness, and utility. Think about the colors of existing plants in your garden—foliage, berries, bark, and twigs—and how those plants and the plants you add will change with the years and seasons. This book will help you through the process of selection.

A carpet of naturalized late-blooming daffodils makes the perfect complement for flowering crabapples.

Double-file viburnum and rhododendrons make a remarkable combination for the shrub border. Their white-and-purple contrast enhances each color, and their similar horizontal branching habit provides unity.

Lily magnolia and azaleas have bloom seasons that peak at the same time. Their restrained size makes them ideal companions in the mixed border with lupines, poppies, and coral bells.

UNDERSTANDING FLOWER COLOR

The purplish-blue tones of California lilac 'Concha' (in rear) and rosemary (in foreground) are a foil for the soft yellow of Scotch broom.

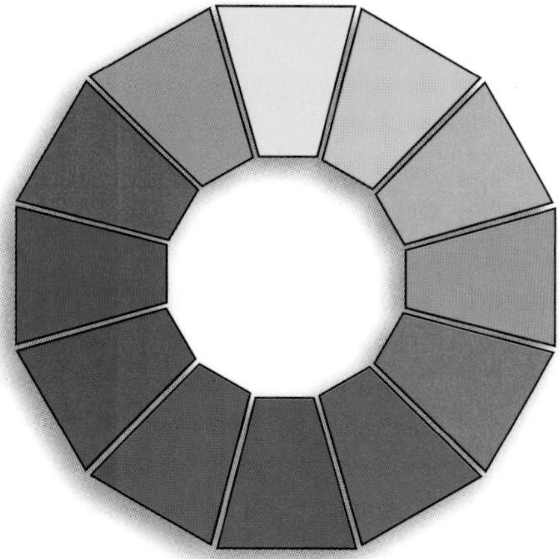

Analogous colors are adjacent to one another on this color wheel; they blend together well in the garden. Colors opposite one another are complementary, and provide dramatic contrast.

Few adventures in gardening offer as much joy as painting your landscape with colorful flowers. Use brightly colored plants and flowers to emphasize focal points in the landscape picture, or to bring foreground plants closer still, contrasting them with less intense background plants and making the view seem deeper.

Developing a theme around one family of colors—combining the theme color with lighter tones and whites—is an effective technique for bringing unity to the landscape. Since white is neutral, it can be used to separate other colors that otherwise might not be fully compatible. Often the most effective color themes are developed around color temperature: reds, oranges—and some pinks, yellows, purples, and greens that have reddish undertones—are warm colors that blend together well. Warm colors are sometimes thought to stir up feelings of intensity and action. Blues, grays—and some pinks, yellows, purples, greens, and whites that have bluish undertones—are cool in effect. They are usually thought of as more delicate and restful.

Color intensity is another factor to keep in mind when looking for compatible color combinations. Unless you are pursuing a carnival of color in your landscape, rich, pure hues of deep intensity are best used with restraint as accents. Pale delicate pastels are usually easier to mix across the spectrum into pleasing combinations.

The color wheel illustrated above can help you identify colors that blend or contrast well. The three primary colors of red, yellow, and blue are separated by the secondary colors of orange, green, and purple. Colors opposite each other on the wheel are complementary; adjacent ones are analogous. Analogous colors seldom clash, so they are safe to use together in the garden. Mixing complementary colors is more adventuresome and risky, but the results are also more interesting. For example, a clump of purple asters is a striking accent in a yellow-orange autumn garden.

Architecture is part of the total landscape. Select flower colors that are compatible with other colors on your property: buildings, other structures, drives, and walks. Identifying the colors of walls, roofs, and paving materials—whether they are warm, cool, or neutral—will help you decide on color themes and combinations that fit in well with your landscape.

Pink weeping flowering cherries provide the color scheme in this garden; red and white azaleas provide accents.

OTHER SEASONAL INTEREST

An important feature of many trees and shrubs is their linear and sculptural character. Although a weeping Japanese pagoda tree *(Sophora japonica* 'Pendula') has no color in winter save its olive-green bark, it makes a major impression with its pendulous habit. Some trees and shrubs, such as flowering dogwood and sassafras, bear flower clusters at the ends of their branches; new stem growth starts from side buds well below the flowering buds. This so-called sympodial branching does not follow a straight line, but proceeds in scallops or dips that resemble waves on the ocean. The horizontal branching patterns that result are interesting even in winter and are accentuated by flowering. The trunks and branches of some trees, such as Chinese dogwood *(Cornus kousa)* and Korean stewartia *(Stewartia pteropetiolata* var. *koreana)*, have patterned bicolored or multicolored bark, and the smooth trunks of old beeches are naturally sculptural.

Woody plants are especially interesting for their seasonal changes. Some color is ephemeral: The flowers of Sargent and Higan cherries *(Prunus sargentii* and *P. subhirtella)* sometimes last only a few days. In Japan, this fleeting quality lends special importance to the drama of its spectacular flowers. In this country we sense this, too, but many gardeners seek almost constant flowering; for them, duration of bloom can be as important as timing. Together, they add another dimension to garden design, making it a puzzle that can be only partly solved in advance.

Trees and shrubs provide a wide range of flowering drama, but they may be enriched with other sources of color. Plants with strikingly variegated foliage can provide summer contrasts, especially in shady spots. Many trees and shrubs have spectacular autumn foliage; for some this is the principal source of color. Colorful fruits provide interest in summer, autumn, and sometimes even winter. Conifers and broad-leaved evergreens, which play a major part in winter just by retaining their green foliage, have many foliage colors, forms, and textures, as well as the range of sizes provided by dwarf and slow-growing forms. Some of the earliest signs of spring are stems coloring as sap begins to flow. Red-osier dogwood *(Cornus stolonifera)* and its yellow-twigged cultivars, and the slender, pale green stems of kerria lead up to the flowers of spring—blooming witch hazels *(Hamamelis)*, red maple *(Acer rubrum)*, and early woodland wildflowers.

Vines offer seasonal effects similar to those of trees and shrubs, and the added interest of vertical planes that can be supported by trellises, fences, walls, and tree trunks.

Herbaceous (nonwoody) perennials offer still more diversity in color and form, and they combine well with trees and shrubs. Because perennials occupy less space than trees and shrubs, they are especially useful for small gardens. Bulbs offer temporary effects that add to the succession of color, and in mass can contribute to the overall garden structure as well.

If you have space for only a few trees and shrubs, include some that are colorful in two or more seasons. See the accompanying lists for suggestions.

TREES AND SHRUBS FOR AUTUMN FOLIAGE

- Autumn Splendor buckeye (*Aesculus* × *arnoldiana* 'Autumn Splendor')
- American yellowwood (*Cladrastis lutea)*
- Flowering dogwood (*Cornus florida)*
- Enkianthus (*Enkianthus* species)
- Fothergilla (*Fothergilla* species)
- Virginia sweetspire (*Itea virginica)*
- Sourwood (*Oxydendrum arboreum)*
- Sargent cherry (*Prunus sargentii)*
- Callery pear (*Pyrus calleryana)*
- Korean stewartia (*Stewartia pteropetiolata* var. *koreana)*
- Southern black haw (*Viburnum rufidulum)*

Sourwood* (Oxydendrum) *is unexcelled for autumn foliage.

TREES AND SHRUBS FOR COLORFUL FRUITS

- Red chokeberry (*Aronia arbutifolia* 'Brilliant')
- Flowering dogwood (*Cornus florida)*
- Washington hawthorn (*Crataegus phaenopyrum)*
- Winter King green hawthorn (*Crataegus viridis* 'Winter King')
- Flowering crabapple (*Malus*, selected cultivars)
- Heavenly bamboo (*Nandina domestica)*
- Firethorn (*Pyracantha* cultivars)
- Mountain ash (*Sorbus* species)
- David viburnum (*Viburnum davidii)*
- Linden viburnum (*Viburnum dilatatum)*
- American cranberrybush viburnum (*Viburnum trilobum)*

David viburnum* (V. davidii) *has unique fruiting interest.

MASS PLANTINGS

'Sevillana' rose massed along a property line.

Trees and shrubs may be planted in mass to delineate outdoor areas. The mass itself becomes the design element. Indoor and outdoor spaces are similar in many ways. In both, there may be floors, walls, ceilings, and places for walking, sitting, and reclining.

Landscape floors may be lawn, bare earth, mulch, paving, or massed ground cover plants. Many ground cover plants provide colorful flowers or foliage. They include annuals, bulbs, perennials, or low shrubs.

Landscape walls may be fences, hedges, or shrub borders. They may be colorful, although excess color is best avoided. A single forsythia in bloom is a refreshing spring accent, but a whole wall of brilliant yellow might be overwhelming. Likewise, a hedge or windbreak of the bluest Colorado spruce would be too formal and intensely blue for most landscapes.

Hedges are usually composed of a single kind of plant, but may contain a repetition of two, three, or more kinds of plants. They may be formally sheared or loose and natural. Formal hedges should be pruned to be wider at the base than at the top, to allow maximum exposure to light. Otherwise, they will become open at the bottom.

Landscape ceilings are formed by overhanging branches of mature trees, or by an arbor or other overhead structure. A bower is a living arbor made from the interlaced branches of trees, shrubs, or vines. A pergola is essentially a series of arbors connected by wooden crosspieces to create an enclosure with a tunnel effect covered in vines. Arbors, bowers, and pergolas offer feelings of enclosure and security.

TREES AND SHRUBS FOR FORMAL HEDGES

Aronia arbutifolia *'Brilliant'*

- Glossy abelia *(Abelia × grandiflora)*
- Mexican orange *(Choisya ternata)*
- Cornelian cherry *(Cornus mas)*
- Escallonia *(Escallonia × exoniensis)*
- Texas ranger *(Leucophyllum frutescens)*
- Nanking cherry *(Prunus tomentosa)*
- Pomegranate *(Punica granatum)*
- Indian hawthorn *(Rhaphiolepis indica)*
- Dwarf alpine currant *(Ribes alpinum* 'Pumilum')
- Arrowwood viburnum *(Viburnum dentatum)*

FLOWERING SHRUBS FOR GROUND COVER USE

Calluna vulgaris *'Walter Ingwerson' and* Erica ciliaris *'Maweana'*

- Scotch heather *(Calluna vulgaris)*
- Carmel creeper *(Ceanothus griseus* var. *horizontalis)*
- Prostrate broom *(Cytisus decumbens)*
- Spring heath *(Erica carnea)*
- Dwarf greenstem forsythia *(Forsythia viridissima* 'Bronxensis')
- Dwarf fothergilla *(Fothergilla gardenii)*
- Woadwaxen *(Genista pilosa* 'Vancouver Gold')
- Shrubby veronica *(Hebe,* low species)
- Aaronsbeard St. Johnswort *(Hypericum calycinum)*
- Evergreen candytuft *(Iberis sempervirens)*

MIXED BORDERS

You can use a border of small trees and shrubs to separate spaces as well as to display outstanding plants. Carefully consider the height and width of each tree and shrub, as well as its openness or compactness, seasonal color, and maintenance needs. For more color, add perennials, bulbs, and annuals. Keep in mind that annuals look best grouped together rather than tucked among the perennials.

HEIGHT: Variation in height makes the border interesting. Place tall plants where they will be seen yet not block shorter plants. If the border will be viewed from one side, plant low shrubs near the viewing edge, shrubs of intermediate size behind them, and tall shrubs or small trees at the back. If the border will be viewed from both sides, place the tallest plants along the center of the bed, with shorter ones closer to the edges. Consider the individual traits of each shrub, as well as its relationship to others. Some shrubs "face down" to the ground; that is, their lower branches arch down to cover their underpinnings. These can be used to cover the legginess of larger shrubs behind them. For example, the leggy tea viburnum *(Viburnum setigerum)* may be placed behind smaller "facing" shrubs, over which its branches can arch, displaying their bright red or orange berries in autumn.

REPETITION, UNITY, BALANCE, FOCUS, TEXTURE: Identify certain plants as focal points in the border and build around them. Repeat smaller shrubs (and associated herbaceous perennials) throughout the border to give a sense of unity, or repeat some of the colors through the border. Try to keep a sense of balance—of colors, sizes, shapes, and textures—although this does not mean repeating an exact pattern. Foliage colors and textures are also important for contrast and variety; flowers don't have to do the whole job. Also consider how the whole border will look season by season and month by month.

SMALL GARDENS: It takes skill and careful choices to garden in small spaces, but the results can be even more charming because of the intimacy of the space. Also, the entire space can be viewed at once. Because you are working on a small scale, you may need to choose small trees and shrubs and to blend or group colors more carefully.

BLENDING OPPOSITES: When colors that aren't fully compatible are used together in a small garden, they can be separated and softened by plants with white flowers, green foliage, or neutral earth tones (such as the warm browns of mulch). Even though green is a cool color, it is usually neutral in effect. When planting trees and shrubs, it is better to err on the side of caution when it comes to color and save bold experimentation for nonwoody perennial and annual flowers that are less permanent.

Mixed borders are exciting when they use contrasting plant sizes, forms, and textures while maintaining a harmonious color scheme.

This simple but elegant border combines dwarf magnolias with tree peonies and rhododendrons in similar hues.

REMARKABLE COMBINATIONS

Japanese spirea flowers echo the colors of the old garden rose 'Rosa Mundi'* (Rosa gallica versicolor) *and provide contrastintg texture.

Like any art, learning to work with plant colors can be a lifetime avocation. But even first-time gardeners can achieve good results by heeding a few rules, then trying different combinations. It's OK to make mistakes (that's one of the best ways to learn). Or you can rely on classic combinations. Here are a few ideas.

■ **Cornelian cherry *(Cornus mas)*** has a mist of pale yellow flowers very early in spring that can be echoed by the colors of early daffodils and yellow crocuses, and complemented by purple pasque flowers, Lenten roses, and crocuses.

■ **Sassafras *(Sassafras albidum)*** has a cloud of yellow flowers a little later in spring. In the wild, it first overlaps the last of the red flowers and young fruits of red maple *(Acer rubrum)*, then the purplish pink of Eastern redbud *(Cercis canadensis)*, and finally the white bracts of flowering dogwood *(Cornus florida)*. You can re-create this combination in your own landscape, and supplement it with narcissus, basket-of-gold *(Aurinia saxatilis)*, creeping phlox *(Phlox stolonifera)*, and evergreen candytuft *(Iberis sempervirens)*.

■ **Callery pear *(Pyrus calleryana)*** has showy white flowers in midspring that combine well with the early pink-flowering cherries *(Prunus sargentii* and *P. subhirtella)*, early white- and pink-flowering magnolias, and the fragrant pink to white flowers of Korean spice viburnum *(Viburnum carlesii)* and its hybrids, accented with forsythia and colorful tulips.

■ **Chinese dogwood *(Cornus kousa)*** has pointed white bracts two to three weeks after native flowering dogwood. To develop a white theme, combine Chinese dogwood with the lacecap flowers of double-file viburnum *(Viburnum plicatum* f. *tomentosum)*, the bloom of white fringe tree *(Chionanthus virginicus)*, the hanging white chains of American yellowwood *(Cladrastis lutea)* flowers, the fragrant flowers of sweet mockorange *(Philadelphus coronarius)*, or any combination of these. For accent add late lilacs, goldenchain tree *(Laburnum × watereri)*, and brightly colored early perennials.

■ **Golden rain tree *(Koelreuteria paniculata)*** provides a burst of yellow in midsummer just past the peak flowering of many other trees and shrubs. Combine it with 'Sunburst' St. Johnswort *(Hypericum)*, the huge snowballs of 'Annabelle' hydrangea, and the white spires of bottlebrush buckeye *(Aesculus parviflora)*. For accent, add pink-flowering summersweet *(Clethra alnifolia* 'Rosea') and the cotton-candy flowers of five-stamen tamarisk *(Tamarix ramosissima)*. Supplement these with daylilies in yellow or purplish shades.

■ **Sourwood (*Oxydendrum arboreum*)** provides the centerpiece for a garden with acid soil. For simultaneous bloom, add late deciduous azaleas, such as the multicolored Knap Hill hybrids and the red-orange

***The pale pink flowers of New Zealand tea-tree* (Leptospermum scoparium) *provide a pleasant contrast with California lilac* (Ceanothus).**

Far left: Chinese wisteria and goldenchain tree make a striking color contrast with similar flower forms beyond the foreground accent of ornamental allium* (Allium aflatunense)*. Near left: The brooms* Cytisus *(in the rear) and* Genista *(in the foreground) combine well with the silver foliage of other dry-soil plants.

Cumberland azalea *(Rhododendron cumberlandense)*. Blue-flowered hydrangeas and perennials such as balloon flower *(Platycodon grandiflorus)*, bellflowers *(Campanula)*, globe thistle *(Echinops)*, and speedwell *(Veronica)* make lovely accents.

■ **Japanese pagoda tree *(Sophora japonica)*** has masses of pale yellow flowers in late summer. Combine it with blues for welcome cool tones in the summer heat. Rose of Sharon *(Hibiscus syriacus)* 'Blue Bird' has azure-blue flowers. Add bluebeard *(Caryopteris × clandonensis)*, Russian sage *(Perovskia atriplicifolia)*, and early blue asters *(Aster × frikartii* 'Wonder of Staffa'). For foliage effect include blue and deep green hostas and ferns.

■ **Franklin tree *(Franklinia alatamaha)*** is one of the latest-flowering trees, starting in late summer and continuing into autumn, sometimes overlapping with its mahogany-red autumn foliage. Other sources of color for that period include the brilliant blue flowers of blue plumbago *(Ceratostigma plumbaginoides)*, which has crimson autumn foliage, and the lavender, pink, and white flowers of heathers *(Calluna)*, some of which have silvery, golden, or coppery red autumn foliage. Other possibilities are chaste tree *(Vitex agnus-castus)*, with spikes of steely blue flowers; butterfly bush *(Buddleia davidii)*, with spikes of purple, blue, pink, or white; and harlequin glorybower *(Clerodendrum trichotomum)*, with white flowers followed by showy fruits in autumn. For more autumn color, combine gold- and bronze-flowering chrysanthemums with deep purple asters.

■ **Japanese and Korean stewartia *(Stewartia pseudocamellia* and *S. pteropetiolata* var. *koreana)*** are natural centerpieces for a winter garden because of their sculptural trunks and striking bark. For all-winter flowering interest in mild climates, add camellias *(Camellia japonica* and *C. sasanqua)*. For late winter flowers, add winter daphne *(Daphne odora)* or February daphne *(D. mezereum)*, hybrid witch hazel *(Hamamelis × intermedia)*, winter jasmine *(Jasminum nudiflorum)*, fragrant viburnum *(Viburnum farreri* or its hybrid *V. × bodnantense* 'Dawn'), and spring heath *(Erica)*. In very mild climates, try escallonia, cape plumbago *(Plumbago auriculata)*, and Indian hawthorn *(Rhaphiolepis indica)*.

***Sandwort* (Arenaria) *is a low-growing perennial that echoes with a finer texture the overhanging flowers of double-file viburnum* (Viburnum plicatum f. tomentosum).**

BLOOM SEASONS OF FLOWERING TREES AND SHRUBS

This chart lists the plants that are discussed in this book by their order of bloom. Scan down the chart to easily find which plants bloom together and which bloom at different seasons. Duration of flowering varies widely, as is shown by the blue bar for each entry. The orange bar shows significant other seasonal interest. Each season in this chart is divided into early (E), middle (M), and late (L).

Plant Name
Sasanqua camellia *(Camellia sasanqua)*
Japanese camellia *(Camellia japonica)*
Hybrid witch hazel *(Hamamelis × intermedia)*
Indian hawthorn *(Rhaphiolepis indica)*
New Zealand tea-tree *(Leptospermum scoparium)*
Fragrant wintersweet *(Chimonanthus praecox)*
Cornelian cherry *(Cornus mas)*
Cape plumbago *(Plumbago auriculata)*
Winter jasmine *(Jasminum nudiflorum)*
Red maple *(Acer rubrum)*
Flowering quince *(Chaenomeles speciosa)*
Acacia *(Acacia species)*
Flowering maple *(Abutilon × hybridum)*
Lemon bottlebrush *(Callistemon citrinus)*
Winter daphne *(Daphne odora)*
Spring heath *(Erica carnea)*
Star magnolia *(Magnolia stellata)*
Sargent cherry *(Prunus sargentii)*
Higan cherry *(Prunus subhirtella)*
Korean abelialeaf *(Abeliophyllum distichum)*
Japanese pieris *(Pieris japonica)*
Winter honeysuckle *(Lonicera fragrantissima)*
Forsythia *(Forsythia species and cvs)*
Pearlbush *(Exochorda species)*
Serviceberry *(Amelanchier species)*
Callery pear *(Pyrus calleryana)*
Burkwood daphne *(Daphne × burkwoodii)*
Saucer magnolia *(Magnolia × soulangiana)*
Fringe flower *(Loropetalum chinense)*
Eastern redbud *(Cercis canadensis)*
Sassafras *(Sassafras albidum)*
Flowering dogwood *(Cornus florida)*
Cockspur coral tree *(Erythrina crista-galli)*
Bridalwreath spirea *(Spiraea prunifolia)*
Rhododendrons *(Rhod. species and hybrids)*
Broom *(Cytisus species)*
Desert willow *(Chilopsis linearis)*
Winter hazel *(Corylopsis species)*
Oregon grapeholly *(Mahonia aquifolium)*
Fothergilla *(Fothergilla species)*
Oriental flowering cherries *(Prunus hybrids)*
Evergreen jasmines *(Jasminum species)*
Empress tree *(Paulownia tomentosa)*
Red-flowering currant *(Ribes sanguineum)*
Korean spice viburnum *(Viburnum carlesii)*
Mountain pieris *(Pieris floribunda)*
Silverbell *(Halesia species)*
Evergreen candytuft *(Iberis sempervirens)*
Bigleaf magnolia *(Magnolia macrophylla)*
Enkianthus *(Enkianthus species)*
Kerria *(Kerria japonica)*
Flowering crabapples *(Malus hybrids)*
Slender deutzia *(Deutzia gracilis)*
California lilac *(Ceanothus species)*
Common lilac *(Syringa vulgaris)*
Cotoneaster *(Cotoneaster species)*
Sweet mockorange *(Philadelphus coronarius)*
Lily magnolia *(Magnolia liliiflora)*
Drooping leucothoe *(Leucothoe fontanesiana)*
Fountain buddleia *(Buddleia alternifolia)*
Palo verde *(Parkinsonia species)*
Tree peony *(Paeonia suffruticosa)*

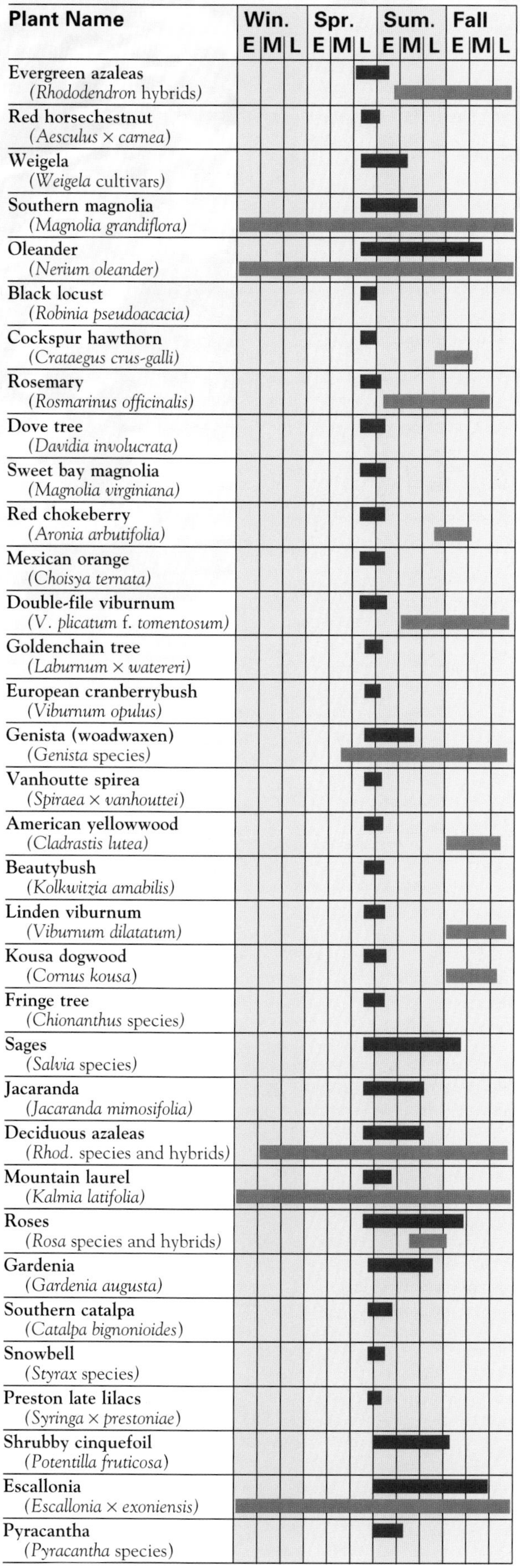

Plant Name	Win. E	Win. M	Win. L	Spr. E	Spr. M	Spr. L	Sum. E	Sum. M	Sum. L	Fall E	Fall M	Fall L
Evergreen azaleas (*Rhododendron* hybrids)												
Red horsechestnut (*Aesculus* × *carnea*)												
Weigela (*Weigela* cultivars)												
Southern magnolia (*Magnolia grandiflora*)												
Oleander (*Nerium oleander*)												
Black locust (*Robinia pseudoacacia*)												
Cockspur hawthorn (*Crataegus crus-galli*)												
Rosemary (*Rosmarinus officinalis*)												
Dove tree (*Davidia involucrata*)												
Sweet bay magnolia (*Magnolia virginiana*)												
Red chokeberry (*Aronia arbutifolia*)												
Mexican orange (*Choisya ternata*)												
Double-file viburnum (*V. plicatum* f. *tomentosum*)												
Goldenchain tree (*Laburnum* × *watereri*)												
European cranberrybush (*Viburnum opulus*)												
Genista (woadwaxen) (*Genista* species)												
Vanhoutte spirea (*Spiraea* × *vanhouttei*)												
American yellowwood (*Cladrastis lutea*)												
Beautybush (*Kolkwitzia amabilis*)												
Linden viburnum (*Viburnum dilatatum*)												
Kousa dogwood (*Cornus kousa*)												
Fringe tree (*Chionanthus* species)												
Sages (*Salvia* species)												
Jacaranda (*Jacaranda mimosifolia*)												
Deciduous azaleas (*Rhod.* species and hybrids)												
Mountain laurel (*Kalmia latifolia*)												
Roses (*Rosa* species and hybrids)												
Gardenia (*Gardenia augusta*)												
Southern catalpa (*Catalpa bignonioides*)												
Snowbell (*Styrax* species)												
Preston late lilacs (*Syringa* × *prestoniae*)												
Shrubby cinquefoil (*Potentilla fruticosa*)												
Escallonia (*Escallonia* × *exoniensis*)												
Pyracantha (*Pyracantha* species)												

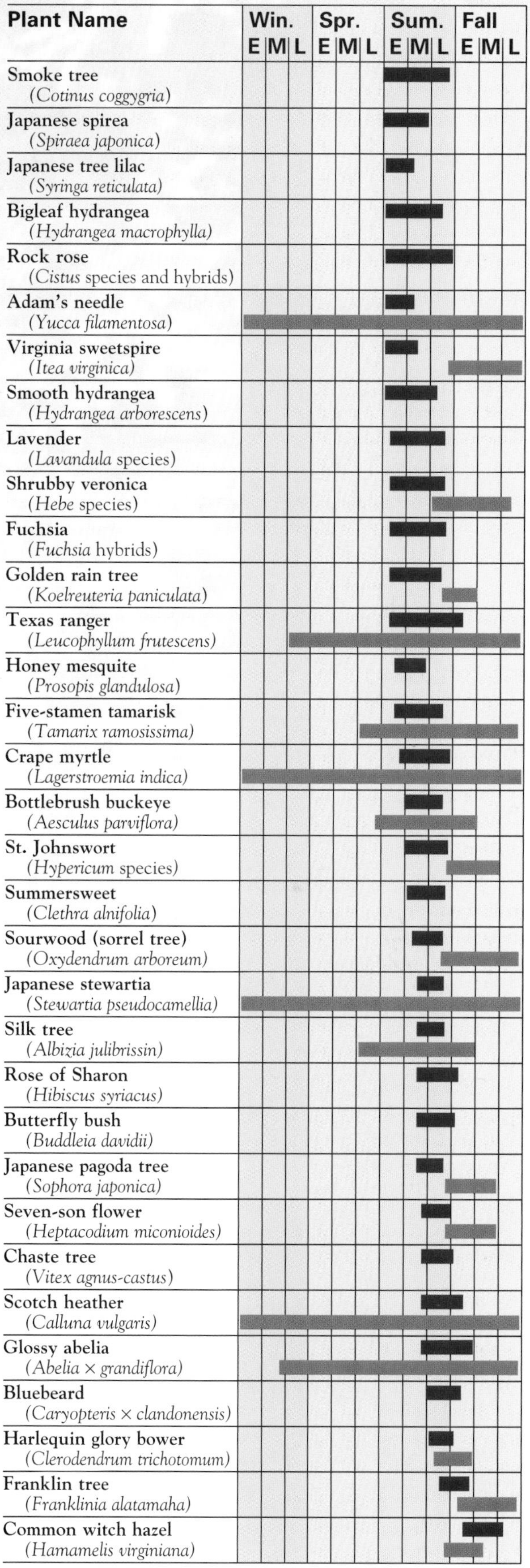

Plant Name	Win. E	Win. M	Win. L	Spr. E	Spr. M	Spr. L	Sum. E	Sum. M	Sum. L	Fall E	Fall M	Fall L
Smoke tree (*Cotinus coggygria*)												
Japanese spirea (*Spiraea japonica*)												
Japanese tree lilac (*Syringa reticulata*)												
Bigleaf hydrangea (*Hydrangea macrophylla*)												
Rock rose (*Cistus* species and hybrids)												
Adam's needle (*Yucca filamentosa*)												
Virginia sweetspire (*Itea virginica*)												
Smooth hydrangea (*Hydrangea arborescens*)												
Lavender (*Lavandula* species)												
Shrubby veronica (*Hebe* species)												
Fuchsia (*Fuchsia* hybrids)												
Golden rain tree (*Koelreuteria paniculata*)												
Texas ranger (*Leucophyllum frutescens*)												
Honey mesquite (*Prosopis glandulosa*)												
Five-stamen tamarisk (*Tamarix ramosissima*)												
Crape myrtle (*Lagerstroemia indica*)												
Bottlebrush buckeye (*Aesculus parviflora*)												
St. Johnswort (*Hypericum* species)												
Summersweet (*Clethra alnifolia*)												
Sourwood (sorrel tree) (*Oxydendrum arboreum*)												
Japanese stewartia (*Stewartia pseudocamellia*)												
Silk tree (*Albizia julibrissin*)												
Rose of Sharon (*Hibiscus syriacus*)												
Butterfly bush (*Buddleia davidii*)												
Japanese pagoda tree (*Sophora japonica*)												
Seven-son flower (*Heptacodium miconioides*)												
Chaste tree (*Vitex agnus-castus*)												
Scotch heather (*Calluna vulgaris*)												
Glossy abelia (*Abelia* × *grandiflora*)												
Bluebeard (*Caryopteris* × *clandonensis*)												
Harlequin glory bower (*Clerodendrum trichotomum*)												
Franklin tree (*Franklinia alatamaha*)												
Common witch hazel (*Hamamelis virginiana*)												

THE RIGHT PLANT IN THE RIGHT PLACE

Deciduous azaleas offer a riot of warm colors, here with complementary cool blues from squill.

Trees and shrubs help to satisfy our environmental and aesthetic needs. They also have their own environmental needs, which we must satisfy before they can perform for us. If we plan well, we can avoid extra work and frustration later.

Selecting plants adapted to your natural conditions is a better strategy than using poorly adapted plants, then spending a lot of time and effort trying to keep them alive. Plants native to your region will usually succeed if you provide conditions similar to those of their native haunts. Many nonnative plants that originated in similar climates can be adapted to a garden. Even adapted plants need extra care until they become established, and no plant is completely care-free. By selecting well, you will reduce stress on your plants, your environment, and yourself.

Mexican palo verde and prickly pear cactus are natural companions in a desert garden.

Rhododendrons and azaleas combine well with other heath family members in acidic, well-drained soil.

UNDERSTANDING YOUR REGIONAL CLIMATE

TEMPERATURE: The primary limit to the survival of landscape plants in most of the United States and Canada is extreme cold. The U.S. Department of Agriculture (USDA) Plant Hardiness Zone Map is shown on page 91. By finding your location on the map, you'll know what hardiness zone you live in. Hardiness zones are based on the average annual minimum temperature. Because this is an average, your zone has seen temperatures lower than the average annual minimum temperature in the past, and will again in the future. Extreme heat also affects plant survival, especially in the South and Southwest.

PRECIPITATION: Annual rainfall during the growing season also affects plant survival and performance. In much of the arid and semiarid West, and in areas of concentrated urbanization such as the eastern megalopolis, water supplies for irrigation are limited, and water use for gardening may be restricted during periods of drought. Even in the coastal Pacific Northwest, many gardeners depend on irrigation during July and August. Because water may be periodically unavailable or conserved in your area, it's important to select trees and shrubs that don't require a lot of water.

WIND: In some regions, wind limits the growth and even survival of trees and shrubs. Wind affects plants directly by breaking branches. It affects plants indirectly by causing them to dry out faster, which is one reason for using windbreaks.

SEASONS: Weather varies from season to season and year to year. A very dry summer in the Northeast or the Midwest is seldom predictable and may soon be followed by wet weather. But dry summers are so routine in the Mediterranean climates of the West Coast that they can be planned for by installing irrigation, or by selecting trees and shrubs native or adapted to the region.

BODIES OF WATER: Weather is modified close to large bodies of water. This accounts for the relatively even temperatures of the West Coast. Areas east of the Great Lakes receive abundant snow in winter because prevailing winds warm and pick up moisture as they come across the lakes, then cool again over land. Climates along the East Coast are modified less than along the West Coast, because in the East weather approaches across land and exits over the ocean. Nevertheless, extreme temperatures close to the Atlantic shore are milder than a few miles inland. For example, camellias grow well on the island of Martha's Vineyard, just off the coast of Massachusetts and at the same latitude as Chicago.

MOUNTAIN RAIN SHADOWS: Windward sides of major mountains receive a lot of precipitation because air masses give up much of their moisture as they cool while rising over the mountains. This reduces precipitation on the leeward side. For example, annual rainfall on the west (windward) side of the Olympic Mountains of Washington is 10 times greater than at Port Angeles, some 25 miles to the northeast. This is called the rain-shadow effect; it accounts for the relative dryness of much of the West and of the Great Plains east of the Rocky Mountains.

PLANT HARDINESS ZONE MAPS

Plant hardiness zone maps are useful aids in selecting plants adaptated to specific climatic zones. Most are isotherm maps based on average annual minimum temperatures.

In the United States, two such maps have been widely used. The Arnold Arboretum (AA) map, published in Alfred Rehder's *Manual of Cultivated Trees and Shrubs* (1940) and revised in 1967, is still used in a few books and catalogs. The U.S. Department of Agriculture (USDA) map, published in 1960 and revised in 1990, is more widely used today.

Both maps are based on average annual minimum temperatures. Their zone-numbering systems are similar at a glance. But they are not identical, and you should be sure to match up the hardiness zone map with the appropriate zone ratings for that map. For example, the AA rating for flowering dogwood is Zone 4. The same area is Zone 5 on the USDA map. Planting flowering dogwood in USDA Zone 4 would invite disaster. In this book, the USDA map is used (see page 91), and all plant ratings are based on this map.

Even though extreme cold is the most important cause of winter damage, it's not the only one. That's why it is important to observe conditions at the planting site as well as noting the region in which it is located (see pages 18–19).

Understanding Your Soil

A good garden soil is loose enough to hold plenty of air as well as water, and is not easily compacted.

Soils are made up of mineral particles, organic matter, water, air, and microorganisms. The mineral fraction varies from gravel to coarse and fine sand, silt, and clay. The organic fraction includes everything from "raw" organic matter in the early stages of decomposition, to humus, which is decomposed organic matter.

Soil texture: Soil texture is affected by the relative amounts of sand, silt, and clay in the soil. A soil well-balanced in sand, silt, and clay particles is called loam. One with mostly silt is called a silt loam, mostly sand a sandy loam, and so on. Soils high in clay are called "heavy" soils, not because of their actual weight but because of the effort it takes to work them. Sandy loams are called "light," because they are easily worked. All else being equal, heavy soils hold more water and nutrients than light soils, yet also hold adequate air (oxygen) if their structure is good.

Soil added to water and allowed to sit will settle into layers of sand (on the bottom), silt, and clay. The finest clay particles will not settle out.

Soil structure: Structure refers to the way mineral particles and organic matter are loosely cemented into crumblike aggregates. The cement is organic matter that has been converted from raw organic matter by soil microbes. The result is a little like the crumb structure of a cookie. Large pores hold air after drainage, and small pores hold water. When the soil structure is broken down by compaction or working it when it is wet, the soil no longer has enough large pore space to be a suitable medium for plant growth. The heavier a soil, the more important it is to dig or cultivate it only when it is neither very wet nor very dry.

Moisture and drainage: An ideal soil for plant growth is about half mineral and organic matter and half pore space, by volume. When the soil is saturated with water and allowed to drain, about half the pore space should be made up of pores large enough that water will drain out, leaving space for air. The remaining smaller pores will hold water against gravity like a wet towel. For all this to work, drainage should not be impeded by hardpan layers, high water tables or, in the case of potted plants, containers without drainage holes.

Fertility: More than a dozen nutrient elements are essential for plant life and growth. So-called complete fertilizers contain nitrogen, phosphorus, and potassium, which are needed in relatively large amounts. Calcium, magnesium, and sulfur are also needed in relatively large quantities, but they are usually present in adequate amounts if the soil acidity is right for the plant. Seven other elements—iron, manganese, copper, zinc, boron, chlorine, and molybdenum—are called trace elements because plants need only very small amounts. Most soils contain enough trace elements, but they may need to be added to potting soils you mix yourself, such as sand, shredded bark, and peat mixtures.

Soil pH (acidity): Soil acidity and its opposite, alkalinity, are expressed as units of pH on a logarithmic scale of 0 to 14. The midpoint, pH 7, is neutral, where acidity and alkalinity exactly counteract each other. When the pH is decreased by one pH unit, acidity inceases tenfold. This affects the solubility of some trace elements, including iron. Iron is the most plentiful mineral element in soil, but very little of it is soluble and thus available to plant roots. As soils become more acidic, iron becomes more available to plants; as soils become more alkaline, iron is less available.

SOIL PH NEEDS FOR PLANTS: The pH at which iron becomes deficient varies with different plants. Most trees and shrubs grow well from pH 4 or 5 to pH 7 or 8. However, acid-soil plants such as most of the heath family *(Ericaceae)*, including blueberries, azaleas, and rhododendrons, are less efficient in taking up iron and may show deficiency symptoms in soil above pH 6. For these plants, it is best to keep the soil at about pH 5.5 or lower. Some soils fall naturally into this range and need no adjustment.

ADJUSTING SOIL PH: Soils can be made more acidic by adding powdered sulfur, which gradually oxidizes to sulfuric acid, acidifying the soil, or by using an acid-reaction fertilizer. Many soils contain free limestone, which counteracts the attempted acidification. Growing acid-soil plants in such soils may be more trouble than it is worth, but determined gardeners have succeeded by building raised beds of commercial potting mix manufactured for acid-soil plants. Even this may not be enough if the plants are irrigated with well water that contains soluble limestone, because some limestone will remain in the root zone, gradually accumulating and causing the pH to rise. In that case, it is necessary either to acidify the water or to catch and store rainwater. These are major obstacles to growing acid-soil plants in much of the Midwest and West.

Yuccas (above) thrive in rather dry, alkaline soil, in contrast with heaths (below), which need a moister, but well-drained, acidic soil (below pH 6.0).

HOW TO CHANGE SOIL ACIDITY (PH) WITH LIME OR SULFUR

SOIL TEST: Test the pH of your soil or have it tested before you start. Then decide on the amount of change you need to make in your soil pH. Next, identify which category best describes your soil: sand, sandy loam, loam, silt loam, or clay loam.

FACTORS FOR MAKING A PH CHANGE OF ONE-HALF UNIT (0.5) FOR DIFFERENT SOIL TYPES	
Sand	8
Sandy loam	16
Loam	24
Silt loam	32
Clay loam	40

RAISING SOIL PH: To make your soil less acidic, find your soil type on the chart above. In this case, the factors to the right of each soil type simply represent the pounds of ground limestone needed per 1,000 square feet to raise the pH one-half unit (0.5). If you want to raise the pH more than half a unit, multiply the factor to the right of your soil type by the number of times you wish to raise the pH by one-half unit.

EXAMPLE: In a 1,000-square-foot bed, to raise the pH of clay loam from pH 5.0 to 6.5 (three one-half units), add 120 pounds of ground limestone ($40 \times 3 = 120$).

LOWERING SOIL PH: To make soil more acidic, figure the pounds of aluminum sulfate or iron sulfate needed per 1,000 square feet to lower the pH by half a unit, as follows: First, multiply the factor listed in the column for your soil type by 60 percent. (If you use fine-powder flowers of sulfur to lower the soil pH, multiply the factor shown in the table by only 10 percent.) Next, multiply the resulting number by the number of times you wish to lower the pH one-half unit.

EXAMPLE: In a 1,000-square-foot bed, to lower the pH of silt loam from pH 6.5 to pH 5.0 (three one-half units), add 57.6 pounds of iron sulfate or aluminum sulfate ($32 \times .6 \times 3 = 57.6$), or 9.6 pounds of powdered sulfur ($32 \times .1 \times 3 = 9.6$).

SOIL TEST: After four to six weeks test the soil pH again to make sure it is reasonably close to your target.

UNDERSTANDING YOUR SITE

'Vancouver Gold' genista makes an excellent groundcover on poor, very well-drained soils, even on slopes.

The north or east side of your home can offer a protected spot for plants intolerant of harsh sun or wind. Here, a 'Scarlet Wonder', rhododendron thrives in a sheltered corner.

MICROCLIMATES: Climatic differences exist even on small urban lots. Consider differences in sun, wind, temperature, and moisture in different parts of your garden. In windy western exposures, plant trees and shrubs that are tolerant of heat and drought. If you have a plant that may be damaged in winter by wind and afternoon sun, plant it in a protected location east of a building or wall.

LANDFORMS AND DRAINAGE: Note high and low areas on your property. Steep banks are usually dry, because rain runs off quickly, so use plants tolerant of dry soil. Low areas are likely to be too wet if there is no way for water to drain away. Either improve the drainage or select water-tolerant plants. Just as water drains, so does air. Cold air is heavier than warm air, so it drains from high spots into low spots, forming frost pockets.

VARIATIONS IN SOILS, COMPACTION: Amend light soils with organic matter, such as compost, manures, or peat moss, to increase their water-holding capacity. You may still need to use dry-tolerant plants on dry sites, or install irrigation. Heavy clay soils should be loose enough to allow excess water to drain through, and should be graded to allow surface runoff as well. They may be lightened by mixing in additional organic matter or a coarse aggregate such as sand or perlite.

LIGHT AND SHADE: Some sites lie in full sun, others in shade, most in some combination of the two. Plant trees to provide summer shade on the west and southwest sides of the house. Notice which areas are shaded at different times of the day and season. There are enough adapted trees and shrubs to keep any area colorful in almost

FLOWERING TREES AND SHRUBS FOR WET SOIL

- Red maple *(Acer rubrum)*
- Red chokeberry *(Aronia arbutifolia)*
- Flowering quince *(Chaenomeles* species)
- Summersweet *(Clethra alnifolia)*
- Vernal witch hazel *(Hamamelis vernalis)*
- Virginia sweetspire *(Itea virginica)*
- Drooping leucothoe *(Leucothoe fontanesiana)*
- Sweet bay magnolia *(Magnolia virginiana)*
- Pink-shell azalea *(Rhododendron vaseyi)*
- Swamp azalea *(Rhododendron viscosum)*
- Arrowwood *(Viburnum dentatum)*

FLOWERING TREES FOR DRY SOIL

- Silk tree *(Albizia julibrissin)*
- Catalpa *(Catalpa* species)
- Eastern redbud *(Cercis canadensis)*
- Desert willow *(Chilopsis linearis)*
- Chitalpa *(× Chitalpa tashkentensis)*
- American yellowwood *(Cladrastis lutea)*
- Hawthorn *(Crataegus* species)
- Eucalyptus *(Eucalyptus* species)
- Mt. Etna broom *(Genista aetnensis)*
- Palo verde *(Parkinsonia* species)
- Mesquite *(Prosopis* species)
- Locust *(Robinia* species)
- Japanese pagoda tree *(Sophora japonica)*
- Mescal bean *(Sophora secundiflora)*

Oakleaf hydrangea is one of many plants often planted in too little space. These may engulf the roses planted adjacent to them.

'Jelena' hybrid witch hazel grows well with little direct sun, and its orange flowers in late winter illuminate dark corners.

every season. Choose carefully, and remember that light conditions will change as your trees and shrubs grow.

COMPETITION FROM OTHER PLANTS: The time may come when the plants in your garden are too crowded. What looks like too much space at the outset may not be enough space in 20 years, so resist the impulse to crowd plants. Areas between properly spaced trees and shrubs can be filled with mulch or ground cover plantings of perennials and bulbs, which can be removed later as the trees and shrubs mature.

Large trees carve out their space needs over the heads of small plants, casting deep shade underneath their canopies. They may also grow many surface roots, competing for moisture with other plants under them. Few plants tolerate both deep shade and drought. Instead of trying to grow shrubs in such areas, it's better to use an attractive mulch, or plant bulbs and spring wildflowers.

SHADE-TOLERANT SHRUBS

- Glossy abelia (*Abelia* × *grandiflora*)
- Camellia (*Camellia* species)
- Wintersweet (*Chimonanthus praecox*)
- Cornelian cherry (*Cornus mas*)
- Japanese cornel (*Cornus officinalis*)
- Winter hazel (*Corylopsis* species)
- Daphne (*Daphne* species)
- Gardenia (*Gardenia augusta*)
- Common witch hazel (*Hamamelis virginiana*)
- Smooth hydrangea (*Hydrangea arborescens*)
- Oakleaf hydrangea (*Hydrangea quercifolia*)
- Virginia sweetspire (*Itea virginica*)
- Mountain laurel (*Kalmia latifolia*)
- Kerria (*Kerria japonica*)
- Drooping leucothoe (*Leucothoe fontanesiana*)
- Oregon grapeholly (*Mahonia aquifolium*)
- Evergreen azalea (*Rhododendron* species and cultivars)
- Rhododendron (most *Rhododendron* species and cultivars)
- Arrowwood (*Viburnum dentatum*)

SHRUBS FOR DRY SOIL

- Lemon bottlebrush (*Callistemon citrinus*)
- California lilac (*Ceanothus* species)
- Mexican orange (*Choisya ternata*)
- Rock rose (*Cistus* species)
- Smoke tree (*Cotinus coggygria*)
- Broom (*Cytisus* species)
- Escallonia (*Escallonia* species)
- Genista (*Genista* species)
- Sun rose (*Helianthemum nummularium*)
- St. Johnswort (*Hypericum* species)
- English lavender (*Lavandula angustifolia*)
- Tea-tree (*Leptospermum* species)
- Texas ranger (*Leucophyllum frutescens*)
- Oleander (*Nerium oleander*)
- Cape plumbago (*Plumbago auriculata*)
- Shrubby cinquefoil (*Potentilla fruticosa*)
- Pomegranate (*Punica granatum*)
- Currant (*Ribes* species)
- Rosemary (*Rosmarinus officinalis*)
- Sages (*Salvia* species)
- Tamarisk (*Tamarix* species)

SITE NEEDS OF FLOWERING TREES AND SHRUBS

Key to symbols:
LIGHT NEEDS: Sn = full sun, LS = light shade, MS = medium shade, HS = heavy shade.
MOISTURE NEEDS: W = wet, M = medium, D = dry, V = very (wet or dry).
WIND TOLERANCE: L = light, M = moderate, H = heavy, V = very (heavy).
PH: actual ranges.
All symbols are approximate; trust your own experience.

Name	Light	Moisture	Wind	pH
Glossy abelia *(Abelia × grandiflora)*	Sn–MS	M	M	4.0–7.0
Flowering maple *(Abutilon × hybridum)*	Sn–MS	M–D	M	4.0–7.0
Acacia *(Acacia* species)	Sn–MS	M–D	M–H	5.0–7.0
Red horsechestnut *(Aesculus × carnea)*	Sn–LS	M	M	4.0–7.0
Bottlebrush buckeye *(Aesculus parviflora)*	Sn–HS	M	M	4.0–7.0
Silk tree *(Albizia julibrissin)*	Sn	M–D	M	4.5–7.5
Serviceberry *(Amelanchier* species)	Sn–LS	M	M	4.0–7.0
Butterfly bush *(Buddleia davidii)*	Sn–LS	M	M	4.0–7.0
Lemon bottlebrush *(Callistemon citrinus)*	Sn	M–VD	H	4.5–7.5
Scotch heather *(Calluna vulgaris)*	Sn–LS	M	M	4.0–7.0
Camellia *(Camellia* species)	Sn–LS	M	M	4-5–7.5
Bluebeard *(Caryopteris × clandonensis)*	Sn–LS	M–D	M–H	4.0–7.0
Southern catalpa *(Catalpa bignonioides)*	Sn–LS	M–D	M–H	4.5–7.5
California lilac *(Ceanothus* hybrids)	Sn–LS	M–D	H	4.0–7.0
Eastern redbud *(Cercis canadensis)*	Sn–MS	M–D	M–H	4.5–7.5
Flowering quince *(Chaenomeles speciosa)*	Sn	W–D	H	4.0–7.0
Desert willow *(Chilopsis linearis)*	Sn–LS	M–D	M–H	5.0–7.5+
Fragrant wintersweet *(Chimonanthus praecox)*	Sn–MS	W	M	4.0–6.5
White fringe tree *(Chionanthus virginicus)*	Sn–LS	W–M	M	4.0–7.0
Mexican orange *(Choisya ternata)*	Sn–LS	M–D	M	4.0–7.0
Rock rose *(Cistus* species and hybrids)	Sn	M–D	M–H	4.5–7.5
American yellowwood *(Cladrastis lutea)*	Sn	M–D	M	4.5–7.5
Harlequin glorybower *(Clerodendrum trichotomum)*	Sn–LS	M–D	L–M	4.0–7.0
Summersweet *(Clethra alnifolia)*	Sn–MS	W–M	M	4.0–6.5
Flowering dogwood *(Cornus florida)*	Sn–LS	M	L–M	4.5–6.5
Kousa dogwood *(Cornus kousa)*	Sn–MS	M	L–M	4.5–6.5
Cornelian cherry *(Cornus mas)*	Sn–HS	M	M	4.5–6.5
Winter hazel *(Corylopsis* species)	Sn–LS	M	L–M	4.0–7.0
Smoketree *(Cotinus coggygria)*	Sn–LS	M–D	M	4.0–7.0
Cockspur hawthorn *(Crataegus crus-galli)*	Sn	M–D	H	4.5–7.5
Broom *(Cytisus* species and hybrids)	Sn	M–D	M–H	4.5–7.5
Daphne *(Daphne* species)	Sn–LS	M	M	4.5–7.0
Dove tree *(Davidia involucrata)*	Sn–LS	M	L	4.0–6.5
Enkianthus *(Enkianthus* species)	Sn–LS	M	M	4.0–6.0
Spring heath *(Erica carnea)*	Sn	M	M	4.0–5.5
Escallonia *(Escallonia × exoniensis)*	Sn–LS	M–D	M–H	4.5–7.5
Forsythia *(Forsythia* species and cultivars)	Sn–MS	M	M	4.0–7.0
Fothergilla *(Fothergilla* species)	Sn–LS	M	L	4.0–6.5
Franklin tree *(Franklinia alatamaha)*	Sn–LS	M	L	4.0–6.0
Fuchsia *(Fuchsia* species and cultivars)	Sn–MS	W–M	L	4.0–6.5
Genista, woadwaxen *(Genista* species)	Sn	M–D	H	5.0–7.5
Silverbell *(Halesia* species)	Sn–LS	M	M	4.0–6.5
Hybrid witch hazel *(Hamamelis × intermedia)*	Sn–MS	M	M	4.0–6.5
Common witch hazel *(Hamamelis virginiana)*	LS–MS	M	M	4.0–7.0

Name	Light	Moisture	Wind	pH
Shrubby veronica (*Hebe* species)	Sn–LS	M	M	4.5–7.5
Rose of Sharon (*Hibiscus syriacus*)	Sn–LS	W–M	L–M	4.0–6.5
Smooth hydrangea (*Hydrangea arborescens*)	Sn–MS	W–M	L–M	4.0–7.0
Bigleaf hydrangea (*Hydrangea macrophylla*)	Sn–LS	W–M	M	4.0–6.5
Panicle hydrangea (*Hydrangea paniculata*)	Sn–LS	W–M	M	4.0–7.0
St. Johnswort (*Hypericum* species)	Sn–LS	M	L–M	4.0–7.0
Evergreen candytuft (*Iberis sempervirens*)	Sn–LS	M	L–M	4.0–7.0
Virginia sweetspire (*Itea virginica*)	Sn–HS	W–M	M	4.0–6.5
Jacaranda (*Jacaranda mimosifolia*)	Sn	M	M	4.0–7.0
Jasmine (*Jasminum* species)	Sn–LS	M–D	L	4.0–6.5
Mountain laurel (*Kalmia latifolia*)	Sn–LS	W–M	M	4.0–5.5
Kerria (*Kerria japonica*)	Sn–MS	W–M	M	4.0–7.0
Golden rain tree (*Koelreuteria paniculata*)	Sn–LS	M–D	M	4.5–7.5
Beautybush (*Kolkwitzia amabilis*)	Sn–LS	W–D	M	4.0–7.0
Goldenchain tree (*Laburnum* × *watereri*)	Sn–LS	M	L	4.5–7.5
Crape myrtle (*Lagerstroemia indica*)	Sn	M	L	4.5–7.5
Texas ranger (*Leucophyllum frutescens*)	Sn	M–D	L	5.0–7.5+
Magnolias (*Magnolia* species)	Sn	W–M	L	4.0–7.0
Flowering crabapples (*Malus* species and hybrids)	Sn	M	M	4.0–7.0
Heavenly bamboo (*Nandina domestica*)	Sn–LS	M	M	4.0–7.0
Oleander (*Nerium oleander*)	Sn	M–D	H	4.5–7.5+
Sourwood (*Oxydendrum arboreum*)	Sn	M	L	4.0–5.5
Palo verde (*Parkinsonia* species)	Sn	M–VD	H	4.5–7.5+
Empress tree (*Paulownia tomentosa*)	Sn	M	L	4.0–7.0
Sweet mockorange (*Philadelphus coronarius*)	Sn–LS	M	M	4.5–7.5
Mountain pieris (*Pieris floribunda*)	Sn–MS	M	VL	4.0–5.5
Japanese pieris (*Pieris japonica*)	Sn–LS	M	VL	4.0–5.5
Cape plumbago (*Plumbago auriculata*)	Sn–LS	M–D	L–M	4.0–7.0
Shrubby cinquefoil (*Potentilla fruticosa*)	Sn	W–D	H	4.0–7.5
Flowering cherries (*Prunus* species)	Sn	M	M	4.0–7.0
Pomegranate (*Punica granatum*)	Sn	M–D	M	4.5–7.5
Firethorn (*Pyracantha* species and cultivars)	Sn–LS	M–D	L	4.0–7.0
Callery pear (*Pyrus calleryana*)	Sn	M–D	M–H	4.0–7.0
Indian hawthorn (*Rhaphiolepis indica*)	Sn–LS	M–D	H	4.0–7.5
Rhododendron and azalea (*R.* spp. and hybrids)	Sn–MS	M	L	4.0–5.5
Red-flowering currant (*Ribes sanguineum*)	Sn–LS	M–D	H	4.0–7.5
Rose (*Rosa* species and hybrids)	Sn	M–D	M	4.0–7.0
Rosemary (*Rosmarinus officinalis*)	Sn	M–D	M	4.5–7.5
Sage (*Salvia* species)	Sn	M–D	H	4.5–7.5+
Sassafras (*Sassafras albidum*)	Sn	M–D	M	4.0–7.0
Japanese pagoda tree (*Sophora japonica*)	Sn	M–D	M	4.5–7.5
Mountain ash (*Sorbus* species)	Sn	M	M	4.0–7.0
Spirea (*Spiraea* species and hybrids)	Sn–LS	M–D	M	4.0–7.0
Japanese stewartia (*Stewartia pseudocamellia*)	Sn–MS	M	L	4.0–6.5
Snowbells (*Styrax* species)	Sn–LS	M	L	4.0–6.5
Lilac (*Syringa* species and cultivars)	Sn	M	M	4.5–7.5
Five-stamen tamarisk (*Tamarix ramosissima*)	Sn	M–VD	H	4.5–7.5+
Viburnum (*Viburnum* species)	Sn–LS	M	M	4.0–7.0
Chaste tree (*Vitex agnus-castus*)	Sn	M	M	4.5–7.5
Weigela (*Weigela* cultivars)	Sn–LS	M	M	4.0–7.0
Adam's needle (*Yucca filamentosa*)	Sn	M–VD	H	4.5–7.5+

TECHNIQUES FOR PLANTING AND CARE

IN THIS SECTION

We see the aboveground parts of trees and shrubs all the time, but their roots are out of sight, perhaps out of mind, and not very interesting to look at. Yet their work is essential to the survival and growth of the plant. Plant leaves convert solar energy to chemical energy as they make the food that powers both tops and roots. Roots absorb and supply the water and nutrients that are needed by the whole plant. In this way, tops and roots are codependent.

Just as plant tops and roots can be viewed as complementary, so can planting and care. Good soil preparation and planting give the plant what it needs to succeed. After that, plant care consists of small adjustments over time to preserve this favorable situation. No amount of later care can fully compensate for a poor start, but careful plant selection, soil preparation, and planting can reduce the amount of aftercare that will be needed.

***Good root environments enable the tops of plants to become parts of magnificent landscapes, as with this ceiling of goldenchain tree* (Laburnum) *over ornamental allium* (Allium aflatunense).**

Before buying a balled-and-burlapped tree or shrub, examine the root ball for signs of breakage or looseness.

ACQUIRING PLANTS

SOURCES: You can buy plants from garden centers, retail nurseries, or mail-order catalogs. Garden centers sell plants grown by wholesale nurseries, whereas retail nurseries grow at least some of the plants they sell and may also offer landscape design and installation services. Most mail-order firms pack and ship plants well and at the right time for planting, and may offer plants that are not available locally, but few sell large trees. Many gardeners buy from both local retail outlets and mail-order firms.

PREPARATION FOR SALE: Trees and shrubs are sold in different ways. Some are dug with bare roots, stored moist, and wrapped for sale. Others are dug with a soil ball, wrapped with burlap, and kept moist. Others are containerized—dug with a soil ball, then potted in a container for sale. Still others are grown in containers—potted as a small plant and grown in the container for a year or more. The method used depends on the age and kind of plant, the season, and the nature of the retail outlet.

SIZE: Starting with a large plant may seem like the best way to have immediate impact, but this is not always true. Smaller plants become established more easily and may outpace a larger plant started at the same time. It's more important to select for condition than size.

BARE-ROOT TREES AND SHRUBS: The best bare-root trees are young; avoid older trees with bare roots. Plant bare-root trees and shrubs while they are fully dormant—before buds begin to swell and expand into leaves. Many retailers buy bare-root trees in late winter; they may sell some bare-root, and plant the rest in containers (which adds to the price) to sell later. Buy containerized plants after they have begun to leaf out, to be sure they will grow.

BALLED-AND-BURLAPPED TREES AND SHRUBS: These are more expensive than bare-root trees, but this is the safest way to move shrubs and older trees. Even these plants lose many roots when they are dug. Some kinds of trees and shrubs are available only balled and burlapped or in containers, usually for good reason.

Some trees and shrubs have special needs. The best time to plant fleshy-rooted trees and shrubs, such as fothergilla, witch hazels (*Hamamelis*), and magnolias, is in midspring, just as the new leaf buds begin to unfold.

CONTAINER-GROWN TREES AND SHRUBS: These plants are not dug, so they do not lose roots, and transplanting risk is minimized. They can be transplanted at almost any time of year when the ground is not frozen. Remember, though, that in the nursery, these plants have received large amounts of water and nutrients to compensate for the small soil volume in the pot. After transplanting, their roots must grow enough to support the growing top under more stressful conditions. If you plant them after midsummer in the North, their roots may not grow much by autumn, so mulch them over winter to prevent them from being heaved out of the ground by freezing and thawing cycles. If you plant them in hot, dry weather, even with normal watering they may be stressed until they have made more root growth. In the South, plant them in the cool seasons.

TRANSPORTING AND HOLDING: Carry plants in closed vehicles so they will not lose moisture in transit. Plant them as soon as possible after picking them up. Meanwhile, protect them at the planting site: Keep them in the shade and don't let them dry out.

BUYING TREES AND SHRUBS AT A NURSERY: A CHECKLIST

ASK YOURSELF THESE QUESTIONS BEFORE BUYING:

1. Is the plant clearly labeled, so you can be reasonably sure of its identity? If you should later find that it wasn't labeled correctly, could you document your purchase?

2. How do you expect the plant to function in your landscape?

3. Is it adapted to your region and site?

4. Does it appear healthy, with a balanced shape?

5. Do the leaves look healthy, not wilted or dried out? If it is moisture-stressed, it may not become established easily.

6. Is the bark intact, without cuts, gashes, splits, or dried or discolored areas? These could be signs of serious problems.

7. If it is in a container, is it pot-bound, with roots coming out the bottom holes and visible on top? Pot-bound plants are slow to become established.

8. If it is balled-and-burlapped, is the ball broken or loose? If so, there may be serious root damage. In any case, lift the whole ball rather than picking it up by one trunk.

9. If it is bare-root, are the roots alive and moist? Open the package enough to see. Keep the roots moist until planted.

10. If it is bare-root, are there new leaves and roots? Bare-root plants should be fully dormant when they are planted.

SOIL PREPARATION AND PLANTING

When planting a bare-root tree or shrub, place it to be at the same depth that it was planted in the nursery after the planting soil has settled.

SOIL: There are two schools of thought on soil preparation. Traditional wisdom has recommended that the soil in the planting hole should be amended with manures, peat moss, or other organic matter to provide an ideal environment for new roots. More recent studies have shown that it is better to plant trees and shrubs in native soil with no additions. Almost certainly, this decision depends on the kind of soil around the roots and the kind of soil at the planting site.

In heavy (clay) soils, plant bare-root trees and shrubs without amendments. In light (sandy) soils, mix organic matter thoroughly into the native soil to improve its water-holding capacity and help early growth.

If balled-and-burlapped trees have been dug from soil similar to that at the site, plant them without soil amendments. In general, avoid amending heavy soil. If you plan to amend it, aim at making the soil at the site more like, not less like, that in the soil ball.

For container-grown trees or shrubs, examine the growing medium in the container, and mix a little of the same ingredients into the planting soil.

It has long been recommended that bonemeal or superphosphate be mixed into the planting soil for trees and shrubs, because phosphate promotes new root growth. Another reason for mixing it into the soil is that, when applied to the soil surface, phosphate does not dissolve appreciably, but remains on the surface. So the only way to get it to the roots is to mix it into the soil at planting. For fertile soils, this may not be necessary, but in a sandy soil or one with a low phosphorus soil test, it will probably help. In any case, it will do no harm, even in considerable excess. To avoid waste, add only up to 5 pounds of superphosphate per 100 square feet of soil surface, or 8 ounces to each bushel of backfill.

DIGGING THE HOLE AND PLACING THE PLANT: Prepare the planting hole before taking the plant to the site. Meanwhile, be sure the roots are kept moist. For bare-root plants, make the planting hole wide and deep enough to accommodate the full spread of the roots without circling. If some roots are very long, cut them back, but don't reduce the full root mass by more than a third. In the center of the hole, make a mound of soil, firmed so it will serve as a platform for the center of the plant, with roots extending radially.

For balled-and-burlapped plants, dig the hole three to four times the diameter of the ball, but no deeper at the center than the height of the ball. If it appears that the mound of soil under the ball will settle, compensate by raising the ball slightly out of the hole. This is a trial-and-error step, but a necessary one. If the collar of the plant still settles lower than the soil level, go back after the soil has dried a bit and readjust the depth. Before the final filling, untie and open the top of the burlap. Trim the excess burlap from the top of the ball and cut away the twine that was used to hold the burlap in place, so it doesn't girdle the stem or roots. If the ball is covered in polyester, however, remove the covering entirely before planting because it will not decompose.

PLANTING: Add fill soil around and over the roots of the plant, until the hole is about half full. Water with a slow stream to settle the soil and eliminate air pockets. Let the water drain away, then fill the rest of the hole with soil. Leave the soil surface slightly concave, to collect rainwater, and form a temporary "dam" of soil around the planting hole to facilitate hand-watering. Water thoroughly. At the end of the growing season, remove the dam, using some of it to re-adjust the soil level if necessary.

After planting a tree or shrub, form a temporary dam of soil around the trunk. Then water thoroughly with a gentle stream.

STAKING AND CARE UNTIL ESTABLISHMENT

STAKING: Most shrubs and many trees need to be staked only if they are exposed to strong prevailing winds. Bare-root trees, evergreen trees, and any top-heavy trees should always be staked to keep them upright until their roots grow enough to anchor them. However, they need to flex somewhat to develop strong trunks. Drive stakes firmly into the ground on three sides of the plant, a few feet from the trunk and leaning away. Tie plastic webbing or other flat material (recycled plastic bags will do, but may be unattractive) around the tree trunk at about one-quarter its height, and tie the other ends to the stakes. The ties should be loose enough to allow the trunk to sway but not be blown over. Leave the stakes in place for a year for small trees, sometimes longer for larger ones.

TRUNK WRAPPING: Trees with smooth, thin bark are at risk of damage from sunscald in cold climates, caused by the heating of the bark by strong winter sun, followed by rapid freezing when the sun's rays are interrupted. Commercial tree wrap, available at most garden centers, insulates the tree trunks from sudden temperature changes and reduces drying. Some of the trees needing this treatment are American yellowwood *(Cladrastis lutea)*, goldenchain tree *(Laburnum* × *watereri)*, most cherries *(Prunus* hybrids*)*, and Japanese pagoda tree *(Sophora japonica)*. Remove the trunk wrap in the spring, so it won't harbor insects.

WATERING: Even trees and shrubs that would seldom need watering after they are established will benefit from extra moisture during dry periods. Water deeply each time, then let the soil dry between waterings. Continue this for a year or so, until the roots have become established.

MULCHING: Most shrubs and trees benefit from a 2- to 4-inch layer of mulch over the ground underneath their branches. Mulch insulates the ground and stabilizes the soil temperature, reducing alternate freezing and thawing, thus avoiding frost-heaving of young plants from the ground. Mulch conserves moisture by reducing evaporation from the soil surface and smothering weeds that compete for water. Mulch also reduces soil compaction and mechanical damage to trunks and roots by keeping lawn mowers at a distance.

Some mulches are organic, such as wood chips, shredded bark, pine needles, pine bark nuggets, and buckwheat hulls. Inorganic mulches include pea gravel and clean crushed rock. Peat moss is a poor choice for a mulch, for it is soon blown away; use it instead as a soil amendment. Composts and manures can be used as mulch, and are also excellent soil amendments, but they can be sources of weed seeds.

FERTILIZATION: Except for phosphate in the planting soil (see page 24), it is best not to add fertilizer at planting or in the first growing season. During this time, trees and shrubs are growing new roots and are not established until their tops and root systems have come into balance. Soluble fertilizers added at transplanting or soon thereafter stress the plants by making their roots less able to absorb moisture. Most soils contain enough nutrients to carry the plants until they are established.

Anchor the new tree's trunk with guy wire in three directions, but leave it loose to allow a little swaying in the wind. Giving the tree wiggle room builds a stronger trunk.

Wrap trunks of trees that have smooth, thin bark to prevent sunscald. Remove the wrap in spring, so it won't harbor insects.

CARING FOR ESTABLISHED PLANTS

Once established, most trees and shrubs need relatively little care, but it is a good idea to examine them carefully at least once a month, to catch any small problems before they become large ones. This regular scouting is an important step in managing pests and correcting problems before they cause serious damage. Good pest management includes noticing and correcting environmental stresses as well as signs and symptoms of disease or insect infestation. Here are some things to look for.

WATERING: Wilting or dullness of leaf color may tell you the plant is under water stress. If you have a rain gauge, you can anticipate this. Most established trees and shrubs need not be watered at the first sign of stress, but when drought is severe, soak the root system slowly until the soil is wet to a depth of at least 6 inches. Dig that deep to be sure. If your soil tends to dry out quickly, be sure to use a mulch to conserve moisture.

A simple rain gauge like this, mounted in the open in your garden, can help you anticipate the need for irrigation.

FERTILIZATION: If you have good soil, fertilizer doesn't have to be added until there is some evidence that it is needed. If the foliage gradually turns pale or yellowish green and growth slows noticeably—yet rainfall has been ample—your plants may need more nitrogen. At this point, a soil test is in order, because symptoms of drought stress can be very similar to those of nitrogen deficiency. To correct nitrogen deficiency, you can broadcast a complete granular fertilizer, such as 10-10-10 or 8-6-4, over the ground at the rate recommended on the package, or you can spray the foliage with a complete liquid fertilizer, such as 15-30-15 or 20-20-20, at the recommended dilution, applying it until some has also dripped on the ground.

Potassium deficiency is unlikely in most soils, but can be checked by a soil test. Trees and shrubs do not need as much fertilizer as turfgrass and will often get all they need from overlap when you fertilize the adjacent lawn.

If there should be a surplus of fertilizer salts, or salt from saline water, you may see wilting without apparent reason, or yellowing between the main veins of young leaves. The same symptoms may appear on plants in soil that is poorly drained, or not acidic enough for the plants in question. These same symptoms can also appear if nematodes or insects are eating the roots. In fact, they can appear when roots are not functioning well for any reason. If necessary, send samples of leaves, and soil with roots, to your county extension service, and ask for a soluble salts test.

PEST PROBLEMS: You may see insects or signs of their feeding, such as leaves with a generally rusty appearance accompanied by light webbing (mites), holes chewed in the leaves (chewing insects), dying of whole branches or trees with visible entry holes (borers), or small, soft green insects clustered near growing tips (aphids). Signs of disease include whitish gray patches on the leaves (mildew); orange spore masses in circular clusters (cedar-apple rust); blackened, dried leaves and stem tips (fire blight); and dying of whole branches (vascular diseases). Some of these are life-threatening, others are less serious, and some are only cosmetic. For many of the most common problems, consult The Ortho Flowering Trees and Shrubs Problem Solver on pages 28 through 33.

Remember that the first and best step in controlling diseases and pests is to use plants that have demonstrated resistance to these problems.

OTHER PROBLEMS: While scouting, you might find mechanically damaged trees or shrubs that need pruning or other care. Or you might find that an understock of a grafted plant has sent up growth and threatens to completely overgrow the variety that was grafted onto it. You might discover a flowering shrub that was labeled incorrectly. Or you might simply enjoy your flowers. Many gardeners have found that scouting is a pleasurable part of living intimately with their gardens.

By scouting (inspecting your plants regularly), you'll be able to discover and discourage visitors, like this root weevil on a rhododendron leaf, before they have done much damage.

PRUNING ESTABLISHED PLANTS

Prune flowering trees and shrubs only if you have a clear reason for doing so. Unnecessary pruning makes it easier for insect and disease organisms to enter the plant. If you aren't sure whether you should prune, waiting may do less harm than pruning.

A good reason for pruning a new tree is to establish a desirable branching pattern. Most nurseries do this before selling the tree, but if you notice crossed branches or too many branches, you can finish the job. Avoid cutting off the leader (the longest or strongest upright stem).

You may eventually need to prune an old shrub for renewal if it is overgrown or has lost its shape. Remove only one-quarter of the main branches and cut back some of the longest remaining ones. Repeat this annually.

When shearing a formal hedge, always leave it wider at the base than at the top, to allow sun to reach the lower branches.

Avoid pruning a large shrub to make it fit a small space. It's better to find the right-size shrub for the space. If it's too late for that, replace the large shrub with a smaller one.

Topping a tree to avoid overhead lines is not a good idea. Doing so will stimulate soft new growth, which will soon become more hazardous to your utility wires and roof than the old growth was. It is better to remove the tree entirely than to top it. If it is in a utility right-of-way, your power company may remove it for you, on request, when crews are doing line clearing. If you plant a new tree, choose one that won't exceed the available overhead space.

WHEN TO PRUNE TREES AND SHRUBS: Pruning deciduous trees and shrubs in late winter increases their vigor, and pruning scars will heal fast. Shrubs that flower before the leaves unfold, such as forsythia, should be pruned after flowering. They will grow normally afterward and probably flower the following year. In contrast, shrubs such as rose of Sharon *(Hibiscus syriacus)*, which form their flower buds in early summer and flower in late summer of the same year, should be pruned in spring.

Most shrubs can be pruned anytime from late winter to late spring. In the North, some shrubs pruned in late summer will grow rapidly and not stop soon enough to become acclimated to winter. To be safe, avoid pruning later than July. Drastic renewal pruning of overgrown shrubs is best done before growth starts in spring, to allow as much time as possible for growth to harden before winter.

HOW TO PRUNE TREES: Prune young trees to select the main lateral branches, if this is necessary. Make all small cuts just above a bud or a side branch. Avoid cutting the central leader of a young tree; if there is another leader of about the same size, cut off its tip above a side branch or bud to keep it from competing with the leader. Take off only a small amount of stem; this will slow the branch down without slowing the whole tree. As trees age, they probably won't need pruning for quite a few years. When they become large, it's usually better to hire a professional arborist, certified or licensed by your state or province, and properly insured against damage, personal injury, and liability.

Eventually you may want to remove a low-hanging branch yourself. To avoid injuring the trunk, use the three-cut method, as shown at right.

To remove a limb, use the three-cut method:
1) With a sharp pruning saw, make a shallow crosscut an inch or two deep into the underside of the branch several inches above the point of branching (push the branch upward so the saw won't bind).
2) Make a second cut a little higher up the branch. Cut all the way through the limb, starting at the top. When the branch falls, the first cut will prevent bark from stripping.
3) With most of the branch now removed, cut through the limb just outside the swollen "collar" of the branch where it joins the trunk. This will allow the cut to heal. Avoid cutting into the collar.

Thin overgrown* forsythia *by removing dead, weak, and tangled branches.

This is the same* forsythia *the following spring after rejuvenative pruning.

THE ORTHO FLOWERING TREE AND SHRUB PROBLEM SOLVER

The remainder of this chapter will help you solve the most common problems you are likely to encounter with growing flowering trees and shrubs. It is based on *The Ortho Problem Solver,* a professional reference tool for solving plant problems. Here you will find the experience of many experts, most of them members of research universities and cooperative extension services of various states.

The photographs at the top of the page are arranged so that similar symptoms are grouped together. Select the picture that looks most like your problem. The small map under the photograph shows how likely the problem is to affect your part of the country. If your region is colored red, the problem is commonplace or severe. If it is colored yellow, the problem is occasional or moderate. If it is white, the problem is nonexistent or minor.

The problem section describes the symptom or symptoms. The analysis section describes the organisms or cultural conditions causing the problem, including life cycles, natural processes, typical progress of the problem, and seriousness. The solution section begins by telling you what you can do immediately to alleviate the problem. Then it tells you what changes you can make in the environment or in your gardening practices to prevent the problem from returning.

In some cases, a chemical spray is recommended as an immediate solution and a cultural change or the planting of a resistant variety as a long-range solution. Be sure the plant you wish to spray is listed on the product label. Always read pesticide labels carefully and follow label directions to the letter.

No Flowers

FEW OR NO FLOWERS

Flowerless dogwood in dark location.

Flower buds pruned off crape myrtle.

Problem: Plants fail to bloom, or they bloom only sparsely and sporadically.

Analysis: Plants produce few or no buds or flowers for any of several reasons.

Solution: The numbered solutions below refer to the numbered items in the analysis.

1. Juvenility: Plants, like people, must reach a certain age or size before they are able to reproduce. They will not develop flowers or fruit until this time.

1. Plants will eventually begin to flower if they are otherwise healthy and adapted to the area. The juvenile stage in some trees and vines may last 15 years.

2. Inadequate winter cooling: In order to produce flowers, many plants must undergo a period of cooling during winter. The plant must be exposed for a certain number of hours to temperatures between 30° and 45°F. The number of hours varies from species to species. If the cooling requirement is not satisfied, flowering will be delayed and reduced, and flower buds may drop off. This is a common problem when plants adapted to cold climates are grown in the South.

2. Plant trees and shrubs adapted to your area. Consult your local garden center or your cooperative extension service.

3. Improper pruning: If a plant is pruned improperly or too severely, flower and fruit production can be reduced or, in some cases, prevented. Drastic pruning, especially on young plants, stimulates a flush of green growth that inhibits flowering. Flowering is also reduced if flower buds are pruned off.

3. Prune lightly, at a time when no flower buds are present.

4. Nutrient imbalance: Plants overfertilized with nitrogen tend to produce a flush of green growth. Some plants do not make flowers while they are growing vigorously.

4. Do not overfertilize plants or make a heavy application of nitrogen before flowering.

5. Shade: Flowering plants require a certain amount of light to produce flowers. If these plants are grown in inadequate light, they produce few or no flowers.

5. Thin out shading trees, or move plants to a sunnier area. Consult the chart of site needs on pages 20 and 21 to find flowering trees and shrubs tolerant of shade.

Scales

BUDS DIE OR DROP

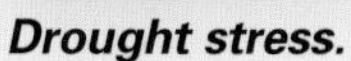

Drought stress.

Bud drop caused by cold injury.

Problem: Many or all of the buds or flowers die or drop off.

Analysis: Buds may die or drop for any of several reasons.

Solution: The numbered solutions below refer to the numbered items in the analysis.

1. Transplant shock: Whenever a tree or shrub is transplanted, it goes through a period of shock. Dormant plants usually recover more quickly and are injured less than growing plants. Even when transplanted properly, however, dormant plants may still lose some of their buds. Plants that have begun growth or are in bloom often drop many of their flower buds or flowers shortly after transplanting. Some buds may remain on the plant but not open.

1. Whenever possible, transplant trees and shrubs while they are dormant. Avoid wounding the roots when planting, and do not let the plant dry out. Apply an antidesiccant spray to plants a few days before transplanting.

2. Cold or frost injury: Flower buds or flowers may be killed by cold or freezing temperatures. Many or all of them either fail to open or drop off. Cold injury occurs during the winter when temperatures drop below the lowest point tolerated by buds of that particular plant species. Frost injury is caused by an unseasonal cold snap, in either fall or spring, which damages buds, developing flowers, and tender shoots of growing plants.

2. Plant trees and shrubs adapted to your area. Consult your local garden center or your cooperative extension service. Plant tender specimens in sheltered areas. Protect shrubs and small trees from early or late cold snaps by covering them with burlap or a plastic tent. Placing an electric lightbulb underneath the covering offers heat for additional protection.

3. Drought: Flowers or flower buds dry and drop off when there is a temporary lack of moisture in the plant. This may be caused by dry soil, minor root injuries, or anything else that disrupts water movement to the top of the plant.

3. Water trees and shrubs regularly. Most plants recover from minor root injuries. Frequent shallow waterings and light fertilization may speed recovery. Avoid wounding plants.

4. Insects: Certain insects, such as thrips and spider mites, feed on flower buds. When infestations are heavy, their feeding kills flower buds, causing them to dry and drop off. Some infested buds may open but be distorted.

4. Control insects with chemicals. For more information on mites and their controls, see page 32.

SCALES

Lecanium *scale on redbud (life-size).*

Problem: Crusty or waxy bumps or clusters of somewhat flattened scaly bumps cover the leaves, stems, branches, or trunk. The bumps can be scraped or picked off; the undersides are usually soft. Leaves turn yellow and may drop. In some cases, a shiny or sticky substance coats the leaves. A black, sooty mold often grows on the sticky substance.

Analysis: Many types of scales infest trees and shrubs. They lay their eggs on leaves or bark, and in spring to midsummer the young scales, called *crawlers*, settle on the leaves, branches, or trunk. The small (1/10-inch), soft-bodied young feed by sucking sap from the plant. The legs usually atrophy, and a hard crusty or waxy shell develops over the body. Female scales lay their eggs underneath their shell. Some species of scales are unable to digest fully all the sugar in the plant sap, and they excrete the excess in a fluid called *honeydew*. A sooty mold fungus may develop on the honeydew, causing the leaves to appear black and dirty. An uncontrolled infestation of scales may kill a plant after two or three seasons.

Solution: Spray with ORTHO Isotox Insect Killer or ORTHO Orthene Systemic Insect Control when the young are active. Early the following spring, before new growth begins, spray the trunk and branches with ORTHO Volck Oil Spray to control overwintering insects. Use Volck Oil Spray only when temperatures will remain above 40°F for 24 hours following the treatment.

PROBLEM SOLVER
continued

Wilting

POWDERY MILDEW

Powdery mildew on lilac.

Problem: Leaves, flowers, and young stems are covered with a thin layer or irregular patches of a grayish white powdery material. Infected leaves may turn yellowish or reddish and drop. Some leaves or branches may be distorted. In late fall, tiny black dots (spore-producing bodies) are scattered over the white patches like grains of pepper.

Analysis: Powdery mildew is caused by any of several fungi that thrive in both humid and dry weather. Some fungi attack only older leaves and plant parts; others attack only young tissue. Plants growing in shady areas are often severely infected. The powdery patches consist of fungal strands and spores. The spores are spread by the wind to healthy plants. The fungus saps plant nutrients, causing discoloration and sometimes the death of the leaf. Certain powdery mildews also cause leaf or branch distortion. Since these powdery mildews often attack many different kinds of plants, the fungus from a diseased plant may infect other plants in the garden.

Solution: Several fungicides—including ORTHO Multi-Purpose Fungicide Daconil 2787® Plant Disease Control and those containing triforine (Funginex®) and *cycloheximide*—are used to control powdery mildew. When planting new trees and shrubs use resistant varieties. Some groups of highly susceptible plants—such as crape myrtles (Lagerstroemia), lilacs (Syringa), and roses (Rosa)—have cultivars selected for resistance to powdery mildew.

LACK OF WATER

Wilting mockorange.

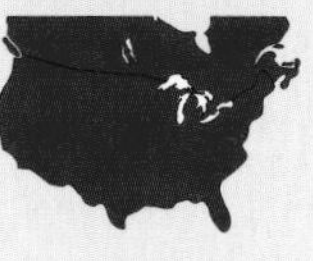

Problem: The plant wilts often, and the soil is frequently or always dry. The leaves or leaf edges may turn brown and shrivel.

Analysis: Water in the soil is taken up by plant roots. It moves up into the stems and leaves and evaporates into the air through microscopic breathing pores in the surfaces of the leaves. Water pressure within plant cells keeps the cell walls rigid and prevents the leaves and stems from collapsing. When the soil is dry, the roots are unable to furnish the leaves and stems with water, the water pressure in the cells drops, and the plant wilts. Most plants will recover if they have not wilted severely. Frequent or severe wilting, however, will curb a plant's growth and may eventually kill it.

Solution: Water the plant immediately. To prevent future wilting, water your plant regularly and appropriately.

EXTREME HEAT OR WIND

Wilting dogwood.

Problem: The plant is wilting, but the foliage usually looks healthy. No signs of insects or disease are present, and the soil is moist. Wilting is most common on shrubs or plants with limited root systems.

Analysis: During hot, windy periods, small or young plants may wilt, even though the soil is wet. Wind and heat cause water to evaporate quickly from the leaves. If the roots can't absorb and convey water fast enough to replenish this loss, the leaves wilt.

Solution: Keep the plant well-watered during hot spells, and sprinkle it with water to cool off the foliage. The plant will usually recover when the temperature drops or the wind dies down. Provide shade during hot weather, and use temporary windbreaks to protect from wind. Plant shrubs adapted to your area.

Discolored Leaves

SALT BURN

Salt burn on azalea.

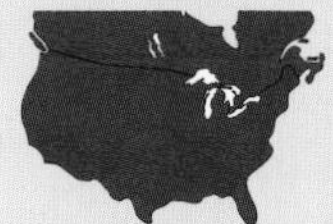

Problem: The tips and edges of older leaves turn dark brown or black and die. The rest of the leaf may be lighter green than normal. The browning or blackening can develop in both dry and wet soils, but it is more severe in dry soil. In the worst cases, leaves drop from the plant.

Analysis: Salt burn is common along the seashore and in areas of low rainfall. It also occurs in soils with poor drainage, in areas where salt has been used to melt snow and ice, and in areas where too much fertilizer has been applied. Excess salts dissolved in the soil water accumulate in the leaf tips and edges, where they kill the tissue. These salts also interfere with water uptake by the plant. This problem is rare in areas of high rainfall, where the soluble salts are leached from most soils. Poorly drained soils also accumulate salts because they do not leach well; much of the applied water runs off instead of washing through the soil. Fertilizers, most of which are soluble salts, also cause salt burn if too much is applied or if they are not diluted with a thorough watering after application.

Solution: In areas with low rainfall, leach accumulated salts from the soil with an occasional heavy watering (about once a month). If possible, improve drainage around the plants. Follow package directions when using fertilizers; several light applications are better than one heavy application. Water thoroughly after fertilizing. Avoid the use of bagged steer manure, which may contain large amounts of salts.

LEAF RUSTS

Cedar-apple rust on hawthorn.

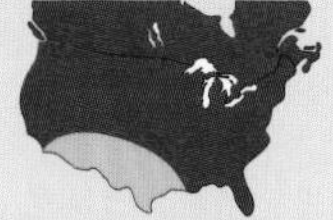

Problem: Leaves are discolored or mottled yellow to brown. Yellow, orange, red, or blackish powdery pustules appear on the leaves. The powdery material can be scraped off. Leaves may become twisted and distorted and may dry and drop off. Twigs may also be infected. Plants are often stunted.

Analysis: Many species of leaf rust fungi infect trees and shrubs. Some rusts require two plant species to complete their life cycles. Part of the life cycle is spent on the tree or shrub and part on various weeds, flowers, or other woody trees or shrubs. Rust fungi survive the winter as spores on or in living plant tissue or in plant debris. Wind and splashing water spread the spores to healthy plants. When conditions are favorable (with moisture on the leaf in the form of rain, dew, or fog and with moderate temperatures, 54° to 74°F), the spores germinate and infect the tissue. Leaf discoloration and mottling develop as the fungus saps plant nutrients. Some rust fungi produce spores in spots or patches, while others develop into hornlike structures.

Solution: Several fungicides, including those containing triforine (Funginex®), chlorothalonil (Daconil 2787®), ferbam, maneb, zineb, or cycloheximide, may be used to control rust. Make sure that your plant is listed on the product label. Some rust fungi are fairly harmless to the plant and do not require control measures. Where practical, remove and destroy infected leaves as they appear. Rake up and destroy leaves in the fall.

LACK OF NITROGEN

Nitrogen-deficient fuchsia.

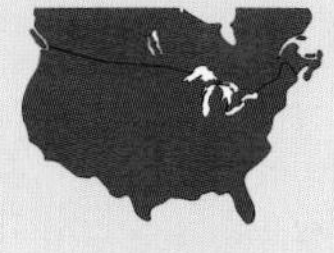

Problem: Leaves turn yellow and may drop, beginning with the older leaves. New leaves are small, and growth is slow.

Analysis: Nitrogen, one of the most important nutrients for plant growth, is deficient in most soils. Nitrogen is essential in the formation of green leaf pigment and many other compounds necessary for plant growth. When short on the nutrient, plants take nitrogen from their older leaves for new growth. Poorly drained, overwatered, compacted, and cold soils are often infertile. Plants growing in these soils often show symptoms of nitrogen deficiency. Various soil problems and other nutrient deficiencies may also cause leaf discoloration.

Solution: For a quick response, spray the leaves and the soil beneath the plant with liquid or water-soluble fertilizer. Feed plants regularly with Scotts Evergreen, Shrub and Tree Food. Add organic amendments to compacted soils and those low in organic matter, and improve drainage in poorly drained soils. Do not keep the soil constantly wet.

PROBLEM SOLVER
continued

Insects on Plant

IRON DEFICIENCY

Iron deficiency on rhododendron.

Problem: New leaves are pale green or yellow. The veins may remain green, forming a Christmas-tree pattern on the leaf. Old leaves remain green. In extreme cases, new leaves are all-yellow and stunted.

Analysis: Plants frequently suffer from deficiencies of iron and other minor nutrients, such as manganese and zinc, elements essential to normal plant growth and development. Deficiencies can occur when one or more of these elements is depleted in the soil. Often these minor nutrients are present in the soil, but alkaline (pH above 7.0) or wet soil conditions cause them to form compounds that cannot be used by the plant. Alkalinity can result from overliming or from lime leached from concrete or mortar. Regions where soil is derived from limestone or where rainfall is low usually have alkaline soils.

Solution: To correct the iron deficiency, spray the foliage with a chelated iron fertilizer, and apply the fertilizer to the soil around the plant. Apply soil sulfur, aluminum sulfate, or ferrous sulfate to lower the pH (see page 17). Maintain an acid pH by fertilizing with Scotts Azalea, Camellia, Rhododendron Food. When planting in an area with alkaline soil, add a handful of soil sulfur, or add enough peat moss to make up 50 percent of the amended soil, and mix well.

APPLE SCAB

Scab on crabapple.

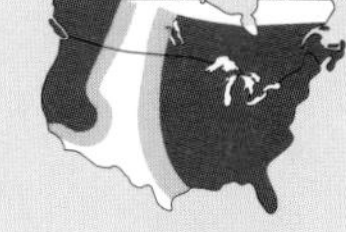

Problem: Velvety, olive-green spots, ¼ inch or more in diameter, appear on the leaves. The tissue around the spots may be puckered. The leaves often turn yellow and drop. In a wet year, the tree may lose all of its leaves by midsummer. The fruit and twigs develop circular, rough-surfaced, olive-green spots that eventually turn corky and black. The fruit is usually deformed.

Analysis: Apple scab is caused by a fungus (*Venturia inaequalis*). It is a serious problem on crabapples and apples in areas where spring weather is humid with temperatures ranging from 60° to 70°F. The fungus spends the winter in infected fallen leaves. In the spring, spore-producing structures in the dead leaves continuously discharge spores into the air. The spores are blown by the wind to new leaves and flower buds. If water is on the tissue surface, the fungus infects the tissue and a spot develops. More spores are produced from these spots and from twig infections from the previous year. The spores are splashed by the rain to infect new leaf and fruit surfaces. As temperatures increase during the summer, the fungus becomes less active.

Solution: To obtain adequate control of scab, apply protective sprays starting as soon as bud growth begins in the spring. Spray with ORTHO Multi-Purpose Fungicide Daconil 2787® Plant Disease Control. Repeat five to eight times at intervals of 7 to 10 days. Rake up and destroy infected leaves and fruit in the fall. When planting new trees, use resistant varieties.

APHIDS

Aphids on hawthorn (life-size).

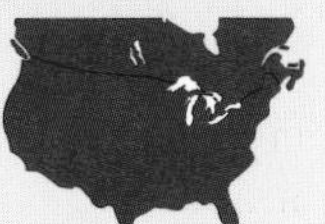

Problem: Tiny (⅛ inch) green, yellow, black, brownish, or gray soft-bodied insects cluster on the bark, leaves, or buds. Some species are covered with white, fluffy wax. The insects may have wings. Leaves are discolored and may be curled and distorted. They sometimes drop off. A shiny or sticky substance may coat the leaves. A black, sooty mold often grows on the sticky substance. Plants may lack vigor, and branches sometimes die. Ants may be present.

Analysis: Many types of aphids infest ornamental trees and shrubs. They do little damage in small numbers. They are extremely prolific, however, during a cool growing season. Damage occurs when the aphid sucks the juices from the plant. Sap removal often results in scorched, discolored, or curled leaves and reduced plant growth. A severe infestation of bark aphids may cause branches to die. Aphids are unable to digest fully all the sugar in the plant sap, and they excrete the excess in a fluid called *honeydew*, which often drops to cover anything beneath the tree or shrub in a sticky film. A sooty mold may develop on the honeydew, causing the leaves to appear black and dirty. Ants feed on this sticky substance and are often present where there is an aphid infestation.

Solution: Spray with ORTHO Isotox Insect Killer, ORTHO Orthene Systemic Insect Control, or ORTHO Malathion 50 Plus Insect Spray when damage is first noticed. Make sure your plant is listed on the product label. Repeat the spray if the plant becomes reinfested.

Branches Die

SPIDER MITES

Spider mite damage and webbing.

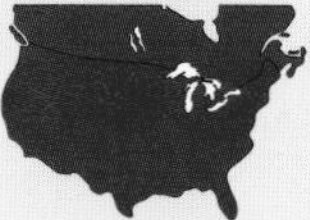

Problem: Leaves are stippled yellow, white, or bronze and are dirty. A silken webbing is sometimes found on the leaves or stems. New growth may be distorted, and the plant may be weak and stunted. To determine if a plant is infested with spider mites, examine the bottoms of the leaves with a hand lens. Or hold a sheet of white paper underneath an affected leaf or branch and tap it sharply. Green, red, or yellow specks the size of pepper grains will drop to the paper and begin to crawl around.

Analysis: Spider mites, related to spiders, are major pests of many plants. They cause damage by sucking sap from leaves and buds. As a result of their feeding, the plant's green leaf pigment disappears, producing the stippled appearance. While they feed, many mites produce a fine webbing over the foliage that collects dust and dirt. Some mites are active throughout the growing season, but they thrive especially in dry weather with temperatures of 70°F and above. Other mites, especially those infesting conifers, are most prolific in cooler weather. They are most active in the spring and sometimes fall and during warm periods in winter in mild climates. By the onset of hot weather, these mites have usually caused their maximum damage.

Solution: Spray with ORTHO Isotox Insect Killer, ORTHO RosePride Orthenex Insect & Disease Control, or horticultural oil when damage is first noticed. Repeat the spray two more times at intervals of 7 to 10 days. Make sure your plant is listed on the product label.

FIRE BLIGHT

Fire blight on crabapple.

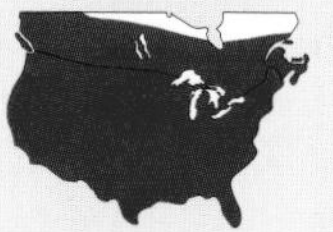

Problem: Blossoms and leaves of some twigs suddenly wilt and turn black as if scorched by fire. Leaves curl and hang downward. Tips of infected branches may hang down in a "shepherd's crook." The bark at the base of the blighted twig becomes water-soaked, then dark, sunken, and dry; cracks may develop at the edge of the sunken area. In warm, moist spring weather, drops of brown ooze appear on the sunken bark.

Analysis: Fire blight is caused by a bacterium (*Erwinia amylovora*) that is destructive to many trees and shrubs. The bacteria spend the winter in the sunken areas (cankers) on the branches. In the spring, the bacteria ooze out of the cankers onto the branches and trunk and are carried by insects to the plant blossoms. The bacteria spread rapidly through the plant tissue in warm (65°F or higher), humid weather. Bees visiting these infected blossoms spread the disease. Rain and tools may also spread the bacteria.

Solution: During spring and summer, prune out infected branches about 12 inches beyond any visible discoloration and destroy them. Disinfect pruning tools by dipping after each cut in a solution of 1 part chlorine bleach and 9 parts water. A protective spray of a bactericide containing basic copper sulfate or streptomycin applied before bud-break in the spring helps prevent infection. Repeat at intervals of five to seven days until the end of bloom. Avoid adding too much nitrogen fertilizer in the spring and early summer. Nitrogen forces succulent growth, which is more susceptible to fire blight. In summer or fall, after the disease stops spreading, prune out any remaining infected branches.

VERTICILLIUM WILT

Verticillium wilt. Inset: Infected stem.

Problem: The leaves on a branch turn yellow at the margins, then brown and dry. During hot weather, the leaves may wilt. New leaves may be stunted and yellowish. The infected tree may die slowly, branch by branch, over several seasons—or the whole tree may wilt and die within a few months. Some trees may recover. The tissue under the bark on the dying side shows dark streaks, which may be very apparent or barely visible when exposed. To examine for streaks, peel back the bark at the bottom of the dying branch.

Analysis: Verticillium wilt affects many ornamental trees and shrubs. It is caused by a soil-inhabiting fungus (*Verticillium* species) that persists indefinitely on plant debris or in the soil. The disease is spread by contaminated seeds, plants, soil, equipment, and groundwater. The fungus enters the tree through the roots and spreads up into the branches through the water-conducting vessels in the trunk. The vessels become discolored and plugged. This plugging cuts off the flow of water and nutrients to the branches, causing leaf discoloration and wilting.

Solution: No chemical control is available. Fertilize with Scotts Evergreen, Shrub and Tree Food to stimulate vigorous growth. Remove all deadwood. Disinfect pruning tools by dipping after each cut in a solution of 1 part chlorine bleach and 9 parts water. Hold off on removing branches on which leaves have recently wilted. These branches may produce new leaves in three to four weeks or the following spring. Remove dead trees. If replanting in the same area, plant trees and shrubs that are resistant to *Verticillium*.

Gallery of Flowering Trees and Shrubs

A mixed blessing of gardening is that you'll discover more useful and colorful landscape plants than one garden can accommodate. Deciding which to use is a challenge and an opportunity. Consider the following in selecting a landscape plant:

Function: This will determine what size and shape the plant should be. How tall and wide? How dense in summer and winter? How fast-growing, and how long-lived?

Environment: What does the plant need to survive and thrive? What temperatures? How much rainfall, and when? Light or shade? Wind? What kind of soil?

Maintenance: Will the plant need frequent pruning? Fertilization? Spraying or other pest control? Winter protection? Protection from ocean spray, road salt, ice, snow, or animals?

Aesthetics: Will the plant be visually compatible with other plants and the existing architecture? What seasonal color does it provide? When? What are your personal preferences?

Cost: What is the actual cost of the plant, including installation and maintenance? What will be the replacement cost, if it should be damaged by storms, vandalism, or the utility company, or if you should decide to replace it because it becomes overgrown?

It is clear that systematic thinking is needed to appreciate how all these variables are interrelated. Remember that you are allowed to make mistakes—plants, like children, have survival mechanisms of their own.

This gallery provides the basic information you'll need to select appropriate plants. You will find more information in the earlier chapters of this book, in tables and lists of plants for specific needs or purposes.

Using the Gallery

Plant names: Common names are useful for talking about plants with a neighbor, but because common names are regional or even local, your neighbor may have learned a different name than you did. There may be no common name that all people use, so common names are not very useful in commerce. Because of this, most nurseries and garden centers use scientific names. In this book, both common and scientific names are provided.

Below left: Japanese snowbell* (Styrax japonicum) *and roses.
***Below right: Pink rhododendrons and flowering dogwood* (Cornus florida).**

ENTRIES PACKED WITH INFORMATION

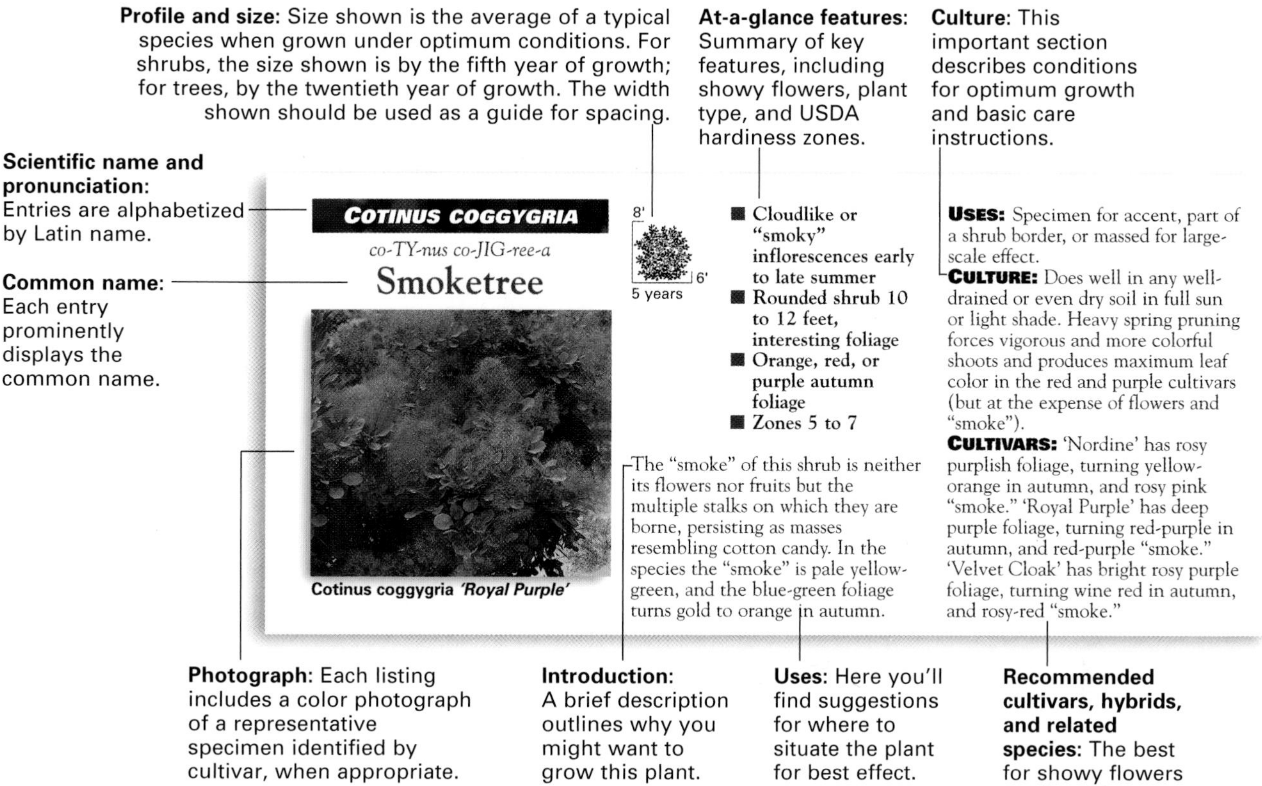

The "Gallery of Flowering Trees and Shrubs" has been carefully designed to pack a lot of detail into a condensed space. So that you can get the most out of the information provided, this diagram shows how the gallery is organized for each entry.

SCIENTIFIC NAMES: Latin scientific, or botanical, names have been used for more than three centuries by agreement among botanists all over the world. All plants are given two names, the genus and the species. For example, *Acer* is the genus name for all maples, and the species name for red maple is *Acer rubrum*.

SPECIES: Species are wild populations of plants growing in their own geographical ranges, and they breed true to their type within those ranges. Sometimes there is a sub-population within the species range, different enough to be recognized but not enough to be called a separate species. This may be given a subspecies or botanical variety name. For example, black maple *(Acer saccharum* ssp. *nigrum)* is a subspecies of sugar maple; Manchurian tree lilac *(Syringa reticulata* var. *mandschurica)* is a botanical variety of Japanese tree lilac. Sometimes a plant will appear that is noticeably different from the rest of the species in some respect, such as having a different flower color. That plant may be given a form (f.) name. For example, the white-flowered form of the redbud tree is *Cercis canadensis* f. *alba*.

CULTIVAR NAMES: The word *cultivar* is a contraction of CULTIvated VARiety, such as 'Peace' rose or 'Delicious' apple. Most tree and shrub cultivars are clones, so they must be propagated vegetatively to maintain their identity. Like botanical names, cultivar names are regulated by international committees.

TRADEMARKED NAMES: Originators of plants sometimes apply for trademarked names. For example, the Red Sunset® red maple is *Acer rubrum* 'Franksred'. The cultivar name is always enclosed in single quotes. The symbol ™ indicates intention to trademark the name; it is replaced by the symbol ® when the trademark has been granted.

SELECTING APPROPRIATE GENETIC MATERIAL: Wide-ranging species such as red maple *(Acer rubrum)*, which grows wild from Canada to Florida, usually show much genetic variation across their range. Red maple seedlings from Florida trees will fail in the North because they are adapted only to mild climates. Likewise, trees from Canadian seed will fail in Florida for lack of enough cold to break winter dormancy. Whenever possible, select plants grown from nearby seed sources rather than from markedly different climates.

ABELIA X GRANDIFLORA

a-BEE-lee-a gran-di-FLOR-a

Glossy abelia

Abelia × grandiflora *'Dwarf Purple'*

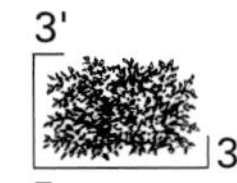

- **Pale pink flowers, late summer and fall**
- **Lustrous evergreen leaves**
- **Fine texture, rounded form**
- **Zones 6 to 9**

This hybrid of two Chinese species grows to 6 feet tall and wide in Zones 7 to 9 but is kept lower by occasional freezing back in Zone 6, where it is semievergreen. Its handsome foliage bronzes in winter. The small trumpet-shaped flowers are deliciously fragrant and borne in large numbers.

USES: This makes a fine formal or informal hedge, mass, or specimen; it is tall enough for screening in Zones 8 and 9.

CULTURE: Best in at least half sun and slightly acidic, well-drained soil of medium fertility and moisture. Recovers well from occasional kill-back in Zone 6, where it averages 3 to 4 feet tall.

CULTIVARS: 'Sherwoodii' is semi-dwarf, to 3 feet tall. 'Francis Mason' foliage is irregularly variegated with gold. A. 'Edward Goucher', a related hybrid, has rose-purple flowers, grows 4 to 5 feet tall, and is slightly less cold-hardy.

RELATED SPECIES: The parent species of this hybrid, A. *chinensis* and A. *uniflora*, are rarely available commercially.

ABUTILON X HYBRIDUM

a-BEW-ti-lon HY-brid-um

Flowering maple

Abutilon × hybridum *'Vesuvius Red'*

- **Large, colorful flowers, early spring to fall**
- **Arching stems to 8 feet tall and 6 feet wide**
- **Rich green, evergreen foliage**
- **Zones 9 and 10**

This mostly South American shrub with maplelike leaves has drooping 3-inch bell-shaped flowers in yellow, pink, orange, red, or white, with many intermediates. Growth is coarse and rangy; pinching out growing tips makes it fuller.

USES: Excellent for informal espalier treatment; also useful as a standard or in a container to be taken indoors in winter. White fly and scale insects may need to be controlled.

CULTURE: Thrives in any good well-drained garden soil of average moisture, in full sun to partial shade.

RECOMMENDED CULTIVARS: Many cultivars are available. A few of the most popular are 'Album', with white flowers; 'Clementine', with red-orange flowers; 'Moonchimes', dwarf with intensely yellow flowers; 'Souvenir de Bonn', with orange flowers and white-margined leaves; 'Tangerine Belle', with orange-pink flowers; 'Vesuvius Red', with fiery red flowers; 'Yellow Belle', with bright yellow flowers.

ACACIA FARNESIANA

a-KAY-sha farns-ee-AY-na

Sweet acacia

Acacia farnesiana

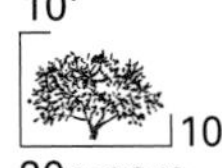

- **Fragrant yellow flowers in early spring and after**
- **Shrub to 10 feet high and wide; tree to 20 feet with ample moisture**
- **Tiny compound leaves and small spines**
- **Zones 9 and 10**

This native of Texas and Mexico has globose ½-inch flower clusters that open in a burst in spring and continue in smaller numbers until fall.

USES: Specimen for accent, or street tree (it is longer-lived than A. *baileyana*).

CULTURE: Grows well in average soils and tolerates alkaline soils better than many acacias. Best in full sun to medium shade.

RELATED SPECIES: There are at least 80 species of acacia in commerce. The commonly planted A. *baileyana* (Bailey acacia, Cootamundra wattle, or golden mimosa), from Australia, has pale yellow flowers. It grows at least as tall as sweet acacia with adequate moisture but seldom lives longer than 20 years. A. *greggii* (catclaw acacia), native to southern Texas, Arizona, and Mexico, grows to 6 feet in the Sonoran Desert, but with water it can be a small tree, with delicately fragrant, creamy white flowers. It is too thorny for public areas.

ACER RUBRUM

AY-sir ROO-brum

Red maple

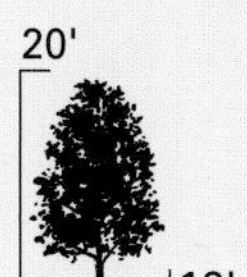

- Small, showy red flowers, early spring
- Silvery gray bark
- Red autumn foliage
- Tolerates wet soil
- Zones 4 or 5 to 9

This usually round-headed North American tree is native from Quebec to central Florida, and its cold hardiness varies with seed origin.
USES: Shade tree, similar to *A. saccharinum* (silver maple) but slower-growing, with stronger wood and less likeliness to be weedy.
CULTURE: Grows well in moderately wet to average soils, acidic to neutral, but foliage may yellow above pH 6.5. Best in full sun but not in windy sites.
CULTIVARS: 'Columnare' is narrow in outline. October Glory® has outstanding late autumn foliage, but is not fully cold-hardy in Zones 4 and 5. 'Franksred' (Red Sunset®) colors early, holds its color late, and is hardy to Zone 5. 'Northwood' is not quite as colorful but is hardier.
RELATED HYBRIDS: A. × *freemanii* (Freeman maple), hybrid of *A. rubrum* and *A. saccharinum*, is faster growing than *A. rubrum*. 'Jeffersred' (Autumn Blaze™), 'Lees Red', and 'Morgan' have excellent red autumn foliage.

Acer rubrum

AESCULUS X CARNEA 'BRIOTII'

ESS-kew-luss CAR-nee-a bree-O-tee-eye

Ruby horsechestnut

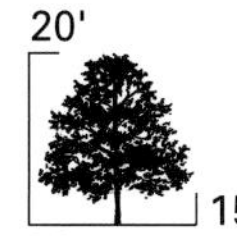

- Rose-red flowers in upright clusters, late spring
- Dark green leaves
- Rounded to pyramidal form, moderate growth
- Zones 5 to 8

This hybrid of the common European horsechestnut *(A. hippocastanum)* and the American red buckeye *(A. pavia)* has the stately habit of the horsechestnut and the red flowers of the red buckeye. It can grow to 50 feet tall and 40 feet wide.
USES: An effective shade tree, but when mature it may cast too much shade for turfgrass beneath. Mulch is preferable to turf.
CULTURE: Amenable to a wide variety of soils, but needs full sun or no more than light shade.
CULTIVARS: The selection 'Briotii' is the best known, but others, such as 'O'Neill Red', are also available.
RELATED SPECIES: A. × *arnoldiana* 'Autumn Splendor', probably a hybrid of *A. pavia*, *A. flava*, and *A. glabra*, has red-blotched yellow flowers and excellent maroon to orange-red autumn foliage.

Aesculus × carnea *'Briotii'*

AESCULUS PARVIFLORA

ESS-kew-luss par-vi-FLOR-a

Bottlebrush buckeye

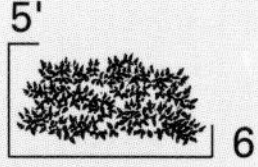

- Showy white flowers, midsummer
- Dark green compound leaves
- Large moundlike habit, moderate to slow growth
- Zones 5 to 8

This native of the southeastern states is a wide-spreading shrub 8 to 10 feet tall. Its 1-foot erect, cylindrical flower clusters appear after midsummer.
USES: Use for accent or mass under high tree canopies.
CULTURE: Grows well in any well-drained soil in full sun to full shade.
VARIETY: The variety *serotina*, from the Deep South, flowers a month later than the species, and is cold-hardy at least to Zone 6.
RELATED SPECIES: *A. glabra* (Ohio buckeye), from the central United States, is a medium-sized tree, 30 to 50 feet tall, with yellow flowers in spring and orange-red autumn foliage. *A. flava* (yellow or sweet buckeye), from the central Appalachians and Ohio River valley, grows to 80 feet tall with yellow or rose-pink flowers in spring. *A. pavia* (red buckeye), native to the south-central states, grows only 15 to 20 feet tall and has red flowers.

Aesculus parviflora

ALBIZIA JULIBRISSIN

al-BIZ-ee-a jool-i-BRISS-in

Silk tree

Albizia julibrissin

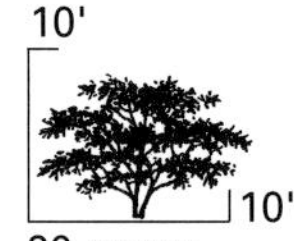

- **Pink "powder-puff" flowers in midsummer and later**
- **Ferny compound leaves**
- **Open, vase-shaped habit, medium to fast growth**
- **Zones 6 to 10**

This small tree from central Asia has an airy and graceful look. Its flowers begin to open in midsummer and continue intermittently until the beginning of autumn.

USES: A single specimen provides accent by its distinctly tropical appearance and foliage contrast. Without a spray program it can be disfigured by mimosa webworm, and mimosa wilt disease can be fatal. It is subject to winter kill-back in Zones 6 and 7, and to storm breakage; after corrective pruning it returns quickly to good form. Over pavement it can be messy with dropping flowers and branches.

CULTURE: Grows vigorously in almost any soil in full sun. It tolerates alkaline soil better than many trees.

CULTIVARS: 'Charlotte' and 'Tryon', selected by the USDA for resistance to mimosa wilt, are useful in Zones 7 to 10 but are not widely available. 'Ernest Wilson' is a more cold-hardy, low-growing form.

AMELANCHIER X GRANDIFLORA

am-a-LANG-key-er grand-i-FLOR-a

Apple serviceberry

Amelanchier × grandiflora

- **White flowers, early to midspring**
- **Red-orange autumn foliage**
- **Edible red to purple berries, early summer**
- **Lightly striped, smooth gray bark**
- **Moderate growth rate**
- **Zones 3 to 8**

This tree grows to 20 feet fairly quickly and can reach twice that height. Its multiple trunks enhance its gracefulness. This tetraploid hybrid has larger flowers and fruits than its parents: A. *arborea* (downy serviceberry) and A. *laevis* (Allegheny serviceberry), both native to eastern North America.

USES: It can function as a lawn or patio shade tree or in a border or windbreak. The berries make fine preserves if picked before the birds get them.

CULTURE: Thrives in reasonably moist but well-drained soil in full sun or partial shade. It has few serious problems.

CULTIVARS: Several cultivars are available, all with good bloom and most with very good autumn foliage color. 'Autumn Brilliance' has exceptional red-orange fall color. 'Cole's Select' has red fall foliage. 'Princess Diana' has showy red autumn color.

ARONIA ARBUTIFOLIA

a-ROE-nee-a ar-bew-ti-FO-lee-a

Red chokeberry

Aronia arbutifolia 'Brilliant'

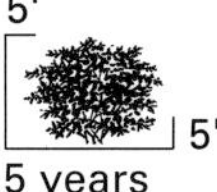

- **Moderately showy white flowers, late spring**
- **Showy red berries, autumn; red fall foliage**
- **Shrub 5 to 6 feet tall and wide**
- **Zones 4 to 8**

This native of eastern North America is found in the wild in both wet and dry habitats. It is one of the best shrubs for autumn fruiting color, and its white flowers in midspring offer quiet landscape interest as well.

USES: Effective in mixed shrub borders for its seasonal color; often used in mass plantings or naturalized in thickets.

CULTURE: Can be grown in most soils, from moderately wet to moderately dry. It holds its shape best, and fruits best, in full sun or minimal shade, but tolerates considerable shade.

CULTIVAR: 'Brilliant' has unusually shiny and bright red berries.

RELATED SPECIES: A. *melanocarpa* (black chokeberry) differs primarily from red chokeberry in that its fruits are larger and ripen black. The variety *elata* is more vigorous and taller than the species, with larger flowers and fruits. A. × *prunifolia* (purple chokeberry) is made up of hybrids between the other two species.

BUDDLEIA DAVIDII

BUD-lee-a day-VID-ee-eye

Butterfly bush

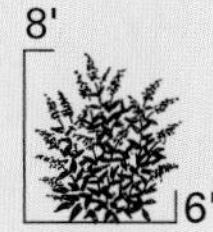

- **Fragrant, showy flowers, late summer**
- **Attracts butterflies**
- **Green to silvery leaves**
- **Zones 4 to 9**

To keep butterfly bush shapely and to promote large flowers, it should be treated as a cut-back shrub. In the North, where it naturally dies back, dead stems should be removed in spring. In milder climates, any live stems should be cut back to stubs in late fall. Flowers come in white, pink, red, purple, and blue.

USES: In a perennial, shrub, or mixed border, it furnishes color when few other plants are in bloom.

CULTURE: Its roots are very hardy, but in Zones 4 and colder a winter mulch of straw gives extra protection. Needs good soil in full sun or light shade.

CULTIVARS: 'Black Knight' is a deep purple; 'Empire Blue' has bright blue flowers; 'Pink Delight' has silvery foliage and large pink flowers; 'Royal Red' has fragrant red-purple flowers; 'White Profusion' has large white flowers.

RELATED SPECIES: *B. alternifolia* (fountain buddleia) 'Argentea', top-hardy to Zone 5, is a graceful shrub 8 feet tall and wide, with silvery leaves and pink flowers in spring.

Buddleia davidii *'Pink Delight'*

CALLISTEMON CITRINUS

cal-lis-TEE-mun sit-TRY-nuss

Lemon bottlebrush

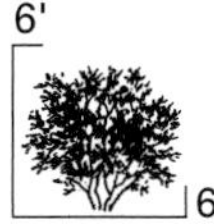

- **Bright red flowers in "bottlebrush" clusters**
- **Upright, with arching branches**
- **Shrub or small tree 10 to 15 feet tall and wide**
- **Zones 9 and 10**

This Australian shrub can grow 10 to 20 feet tall. Its 2- to 5-inch spikes of bright red flowers are borne in quantity in spring and summer, fewer later. Its narrow blue-green leaves are stiffly leathery, and have a citrus odor when crushed.

USES: Makes a good hedge or screen with pruning for fullness.

CULTURE: Grows in any well-drained soil, better dry than moist, and with good air circulation to deter disease, especially in humid climates. It is tolerant of alkaline and saline soils and hot climates. Best in full sun.

CULTIVARS: 'Jeffersii' has pink flowers. 'Splendens' has larger red flowers.

RELATED SPECIES: Two smaller species are more cold-hardy, perhaps to Zone 8. *C. salignus* var. *viridiflorus* (Tasmanian bottlebrush) has yellow-green flowers and is more tolerant of wet soils. *C. sieberi* (alpine bottlebrush), from higher elevations in Australia, has creamy yellow flowers.

Callistemon citrinus

CALLUNA VULGARIS

ka-LOON-a vul-GARE-iss

Scotch heather

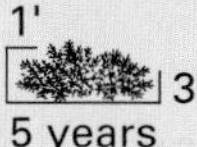

- **Carpet of flowers in late summer or early autumn**
- **Evergreen ground-cover shrub**
- **Varied foliage colors**
- **Zones 6 and 7, and Zone 5 with reliable snow cover**

This shrub has the flowering effect of the spring heaths *(Erica)*, but in late summer and autumn. Flower and foliage colors vary.

USES: Ground cover or for special effect in a border with acidic soil.

CULTURE: Best in perfectly drained, peaty soils, low in fertility and acidic (below pH 5.5). Flowers well only in full sun. Benefits from a light cover of evergreen boughs over winter during establishment.

CULTIVARS: Many variants are available. 'Alba Aurea' has white flowers and gray-green foliage. 'Aurea' and 'Cuprea' have golden foliage, bronzing in winter; 'Blazeaway' has golden foliage in spring, turning red to orange in winter, and lilac flowers. 'Corbett's Red' has deep rose-pink flowers. 'County Wicklow' has double lavender-pink flowers over a long period in summer. 'H.E. Beale' has double silvery pink flowers, late. 'J.H. Hamilton' has double salmon-pink flowers. 'Mrs. Ronald Gray' has rosy-pink flowers and grows only 4 inches tall.

Calluna vulgaris *'Peter Sparkes'*

CAMELLIA JAPONICA

ka-MEAL-ee-a ja-PON-i-ka

Japanese camellia

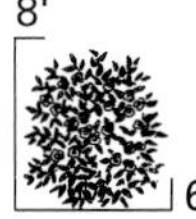

- Showy flowers, early winter to early spring
- Lustrous evergreen foliage
- Zones 8 to 10, milder parts of Zone 7

This beloved tea relative from China and Japan has been widely planted in the Deep South and the West Coast. Its elegant white, pink, and red flowers are accompanied by smooth, leathery evergreen leaves. This stately pyramidal shrub or tree grows slowly to 20 feet tall, very old plants to 40 feet.

USE: Fine as a specimen or a screen planting on large sites.
CULTURE: Best in acidic soil rich in organic matter, where it rarely needs fertilization. Flowers best in full sun but winters best with light shade. Sites that are windy, especially in winter, should be avoided. It is shallow-rooted and should be mulched, and vehicles kept away, so as not to compact the soil. Scale insects may need to be controlled, and it may need occasional watering during very dry periods.
CULTIVARS: At least 200 selections are available. Choices will usually be based on flower character and local availability, but a few popular ones are 'Debutante', with double light pink flowers, opening early; 'Kumasaka', with double bright rose-pink flowers, opening late; 'Pink Perfection' ('Otome'), with small, formal, double pale shell-pink flowers, over a long bloom season; and 'Prof. Charles S. Sargent', with double dark red flowers and a compact upright habit.
RELATED SPECIES AND HYBRIDS: *C. sasanqua* (sasanqua camellia) has similar but slightly smaller leaves and flowers and makes a more effective screen. Its flowers come in the same color range as those of Japanese camellia but open from autumn to early winter. Many cultivars are available, including 'Bonanza', with semidouble scarlet flowers showing bright yellow stamens; 'Chansonette', with formal, double bright rose-pink flowers and a cascading habit; and 'Mine-no-yuki' ('White Dove'), with attractive semidouble white flowers. *C. oleifera* (oil-bearing camellia) is a parent of a new group of hardier hybrids introduced by the U.S. National Arboretum. C. 'Polar Ice', 'Snow Flurry', 'Winter's Hope', and 'Winter's Waterlily' have white flowers; 'Winter's Dream' and 'Winter's Rose' have pink flowers; 'Winter's Charm' and 'Winter's Interlude' have lavender-pink flowers; and 'Winter's Star' has reddish-pink flowers. All are hardy in Zone 7 and may prove to be in Zone 6 as well.

Camellia japonica *'Debutante'*

Camellia sasanqua *'Narumi-gata'*

CARYOPTERIS X CLANDONENSIS

care-ee-OP-ter-iss clan-dun-EN-sis

Bluebeard

Caryopteris × clandonensis *'Longwood Blue'*

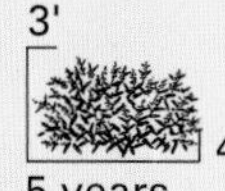

- Blue flowers, late summer
- Gray-green foliage
- Airy, graceful habit
- Zones 4 to 8

This cut-back shrub from eastern Asia should be pruned back to 4- to 6-inch stubs each spring to maintain its shape and promote heavy flowering the following summer. When treated this way, it will grow 3 to 4 feet tall and at least as broad in a single season, once it is established. It is an excellent source of blue color at a rather dull season, and it combines well with herbaceous plants having late summer color.

USES: In the shrub border, for blue flowers in late summer; also fine as a specimen.
CULTURE: Troublefree; performs well in any well-drained garden soil in full sun to light shade.
CULTIVARS: The oldest selection, 'Blue Mist', has soft blue flowers, opening early. 'Dark Knight' is lower growing, with silvery green leaves and deep blue flowers. 'Longwood Blue' has bright blue flowers, opening over a long period. 'Worcester Gold' has yellow foliage and blue flowers.

CATALPA BIGNONIOIDES

ka-TAL-pa big-know-nee-EYE-dees

Southern catalpa

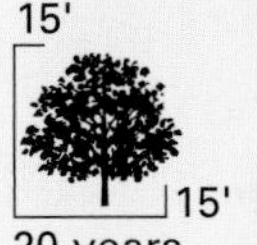

- Showy clusters of white flowers, early summer
- Moderately fast growth
- Large bright green leaves
- Zones 5 to 9

This tropical-looking tree, to 30 feet tall and at least as wide, has large heart-shaped leaves, 3 to 6 inches long and wide, and trumpet-shaped white flowers with yellow and brown throat markings. Long, hanging pods can litter the ground.

USES: Best planted to be seen at some distance and where its leaf and pod litter is not troublesome.

CULTURE: Tolerates most environmental extremes but needs full sun to flower well.

CULTIVARS: 'Aurea' has striking yellow leaves in spring that turn green by midsummer. 'Nana' is a dwarf form, usually grafted in a standard (erect trunk) for display as a small globe or umbrella.

RELATED SPECIES: C. *ovata* (Northern or Western catalpa) is narrower and much taller, 60 to 80 feet, with flowering and foliage similar to that of Southern catalpa. It flowers a week or two later. C. *fargesii*, from western China, has smaller leaves and yellow- and brown-spotted rose-pink flowers. It is useful in Zones 6 to 9.

Catalpa bignonioides

CEANOTHUS SPECIES AND HYBRIDS

see-a-NO-thuss

California lilac

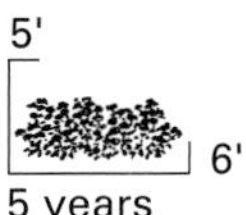

- Fragrant azure-blue flowers (some species), in spring
- Adapted to the West Coast
- Dark evergreen leaves
- Zones 8 to 10

These natives of coastal Mexico and California are not really lilacs but remarkable shrubs in their own right, with clusters of blue flowers (white and pink in some species) and glossy, handsomely textured leaves, making a full mass.

USES: The blue-flowered cultivars vary from 2-foot ground covers to large shrubs. Taller ones make excellent hedges.

CULTURE: These plants tolerate dry conditions and do not respond well to too much irrigation. They should not remain wet for long. They perform well only in Pacific coastal areas. Plant in full sun.

RELATED SPECIES: Most blue ceanothus are selections of C. *gloriosus* (Point Reyes ceanothus), C. *griseus* var. *horizontalis* (Carmel creeper), C. *impressus* (Santa Barbara ceanothus), or hybrids of these. Deciduous white-flowered *Ceanothus* species native to eastern North America are more cold-hardy but lack landscape appeal.

Ceanothus impressus

CERCIS CANADENSIS

SIR-sis can-a DEN-sis

Eastern redbud

- Purplish pink, clear pink, or white flowers before leaves unfold
- Small tree (15 to 25 feet), moderate growth
- Heart-shaped leaves turn yellow in autumn
- Zones 5 to 9

At the extremes of its wide range, from the eastern states to Florida and Mexico, it's best to use native material or cultivars adapted to the region.

USES: Patio tree, small shade or street tree, naturalizing.

CULTURE: Adaptable to any well-drained garden soil even though dry. Flowers well in full sun or considerable shade. Maintenance is minimal.

CULTIVARS: The form *Cercis canadensis* f. *alba* and the cultivar 'Royal White' have pure white flowers. 'Flame' has large, double flowers and great vigor. 'Forest Pansy' has deep red-purple leaves that fade to bronze in summer. 'Pinkbud' and 'Wither's Pink Charm' have clear bright-pink flowers. 'Rubye Atkinson' has soft pink flowers.

RELATED SPECIES: C. *chinensis* (Chinese redbud) is shrubby in habit, seldom over 15 feet tall in Zones 6 and 7, 30 feet tall in milder climates, and has larger, deep rosy-purple flowers.

Cercis canadensis

CHAENOMELES SPECIOSA

kee-NOM-el-eez spee-see-OH-sa

Flowering quince

Chaenomeles speciosa

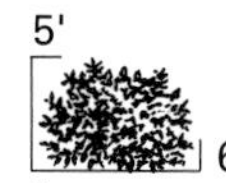

- **Showy flowers, early spring**
- **Tall shrub (most are above 5 feet tall)**
- **Dense and thorny**
- **Zones 5 to 9**

Red, pink, or white flowers open with those of forsythia.

USES: Border, specimen, or barrier.

CULTURE: Needs full sun for best flowering. Tolerates moderately wet or dry soil and windy sites.

CULTIVARS: 'Apple Blossom' has pale pink flowers; 'Nivalis', pure white; 'Spit Fire', bright red; and 'Toyo Nishiki' white, pink, and red flowers on the same plant.

RELATED SPECIES: *C. japonica* (Japanese flowering quince) seldom grows above 3 feet. 'Orange Delight' has orange flowers; 'Rubra' has deep red flowers. 'Minerva', a hybrid of *C. japonica* and *C. cathayensis*, has cherry-red flowers and is cold-hardy only to Zone 6. *C.* × *superba* includes medium-height hybrids between *C. japonica* and *C. speciosa:* 'Cameo' has apricot-pink flowers on a thornless plant; 'Texas Scarlet', profuse cherry-red flowers, and 'Jet Trail', white flowers. *C.* × *californica* includes hybrids of *C.* × *superba* 'Corallina' by the more tender *C. cathayensis*. Of these, 'Pink Beauty', with rose-pink flowers, remains popular.

CHILOPSIS LINEARIS

kyle-OP-sis lin-e-AIR-iss

Desert willow

Chilopsis linearis *'Burgundy'*

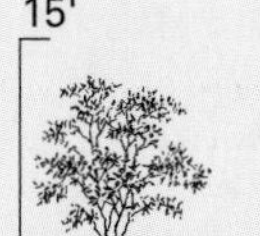

- **Purple-tinted white flowers in late spring**
- **Fast-growing tree to 20 feet**
- **Long, narrow leaves drop early**
- **Zones 8 and 9**

This shrubby tree from Texas, Mexico, and Southern California has flowers similar to but smaller than those of the closely related catalpa.

USES: Small graceful patio tree with willowlike foliage. Holds its pencil-like fruits over winter, then looks shaggy. Pruning improves form. Flowers attract hummingbirds.

CULTURE: Needs water for establishment, then tolerates long dry periods. Flowers best in full sun and performs well in poor soil.

CULTIVAR: 'Burgundy' has fragrant deep red-purple flowers.

RELATED SPECIES: × *Chitalpa tashkentensis* (chitalpa) is a hybrid between *Catalpa bignonioides* and *Chilopsis linearis* made at the Taskent Botanical Garden of the Uzbek Republic. It grows 20 to 30 feet tall and bears pink flowers from late spring to early fall. Two clones have been named at the Rancho Santa Ana Botanical Garden: 'Pink Dawn' has a spreading habit and light pink flowers; 'Morning Cloud' is more vigorous and more upright, with pale pink to white flowers.

CHIMONANTHUS PRAECOX

kye-mon-ANN-thuss PRE-cox

Fragrant wintersweet

Chimonanthus praecox *'Luteus'*

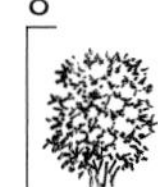

- **Fragrant yellow flowers, late winter or early spring**
- **Shrub to 10 feet tall and wide**
- **Lustrous dark green foliage**
- **Zones 8 and 9**

This large shrub from China is most notable for its fragrant, 1-inch pale yellow flowers with deep red-brown centers in late winter (Zones 9+) or early spring (Zone 8 and mildest Zone 7). It also has handsome leaves, 3 to 6 inches long, after flowering and until autumn.

USES: Specimen, screen, or back of shrub border. Works well as an espalier against an east- or north-facing wall. In maritime sites where summers are moderate, it will grow well against a south-facing wall.

CULTURE: Thrives in somewhat wet to average acidic soil and full sun to considerable shade. Where summers are hot, it should be shaded. Needs little care except for pruning out deadwood and, eventually, renewal pruning.

CULTIVARS: 'Grandiflorus' has larger leaves to 8 inches long, and larger but less fragrant pure yellow flowers with deep red centers. 'Luteus' has large, clear, pale yellow flowers, opening later than the species.

CHIONANTHUS VIRGINICUS

kio-NAN-thuss ver-JIN-i-cus

White fringe tree

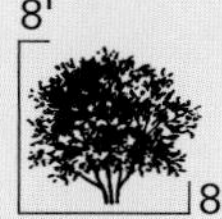

- Fringelike white flowers, late spring
- Large shrub, almost treelike
- Leaves turn pale yellow in fall
- Blue-black fruits, autumn
- Zones 5 to 9, parts of Zone 4

This southeastern native and member of the olive family *(Oleaceae)* grows 12 to 15 feet tall and wide and bears showy white flowers in late spring (male plants bear showier flowers than females). Female plants bear blue-black fruits resembling small olives.

USES: Specimen or back of the shrub border.

CULTURE: Thrives in any good garden soil; flowers best in full sun.

RELATED SPECIES: *C. retusus* (Chinese fringe tree), from Asia, is shaped like a miniature American elm tree, grows 15 to 20 feet tall, and is useful in Zones 6 to 9. Its clusters of fringelike white flowers are smaller than those of white fringe tree and appear a little later. The variety *serrulatus*, from Taiwan, is a low-branching tree with exfoliating cinnamon-brown bark on young branches and a coarsely striped trunk. It is cold-hardy in Zones 7 to 9 and parts of Zone 6.

Chionanthus virginicus

CHOISYA TERNATA

cho-EEZ-ya ter-NATE-a

Mexican orange

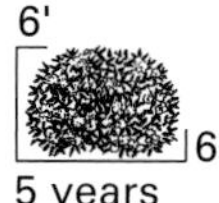

- Fragrant white flowers in showy clusters, late spring
- Glossy dark green 3-leaflet leaves are aromatic
- Tolerant of dry soils
- Zones 9 and 10; Zone 8 with protection

This large shrub from Mexico grows to 8 feet in time, its compact mass of evergreen foliage enhanced by the fragrant flowers in late spring.

USES: Visual screen or barrier, as a specimen, or in a shrub border.

CULTURE: Best in full sun where summers are cool, but needs light shade in hot summers. Good soil preparation is important: alkaline or saline soils are not recommended. Established in a good site, it may need pruning only for rejuvenation, and a sharp eye for insect problems.

CULTIVARS: 'Sundance' has golden to lime-green foliage.

RELATED SPECIES: *Poncirus trifoliata* (hardy orange), a small shrubby tree from China and Korea, is loose and open in habit with small deciduous leaves and stout green stems covered with large thorns. It is one of the most effective barrier plants. It has fragrant white flowers similar to those of the closely related *Citrus* species, and its fruits are 1- to 2-inch sour oranges, marginally edible.

Choisya ternata

CISTUS SPECIES AND HYBRIDS

SIS-tus

Rock rose

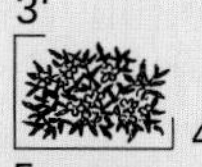

- Many-colored flowers, summer
- Shrubs 3 to 6 feet tall
- Aromatic foliage
- Tolerant of dry soil, wind, and salt
- Zones 8 to 10

These plants offer a variety of flower and foliage colors in summer.

USES: Specimens for accent, massing, front of the shrub border.

CULTURE: Pot-grown plants are recommended; others are difficult to transplant. Properly sited and established, they require little maintenance.

SPECIES AND CULTIVARS: *C. incanus* (hairy rock rose), to 3 feet tall, has rose to purple, yellow-centered flowers; its hybrid, 'Silver Pink', has light pink flowers and silvery foliage. *C. laurifolius* (laurel rock rose), probably the hardiest species, grows 5 feet tall and has white flowers with yellow centers and leathery dark green foliage, smooth on top. 'Peggy Sammons' is a popular hybrid of *C. laurifolius*, to 3 feet tall, with rose-pink flowers and gray-green foliage. *Cistus salviifolius* (sage rock rose) has net-veined, sage-green leaves and 2-inch white flowers with yellow throats.

Cistus × purpureus

CLADRASTIS LUTEA (C. KENTUKEA)

cla-DRAS-tis LOOT-ee-a

American yellowwood

Cladrastis lutea

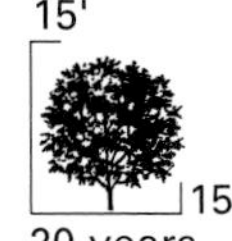

- **Hanging chains of fragrant white flowers, late spring**
- **Dark green leaves turning golden yellow in autumn**
- **Smooth-sculpted light gray bark**
- **Zones 5 to 8**

This native tree from the mountains of North Carolina to Missouri grows 30 to 40 feet tall and wide with a rounded crown. Its hanging clusters of pealike white flowers resemble white wisteria blooms, but it does not flower fully every year. Golden fall foliage, sculpted trunk, and light gray bark round out its seasonal interest. Its heavy, dark green foliage canopy casts deep shade.

USES: Effective shade tree but may need careful pruning to eliminate pocketlike branch crotches where water can collect and decay may start.

CULTURE: Performs well in just about any well-drained soil; fine in alkaline soils. Flowers best in full sun.

RELATED SPECIES: *Maackia amurensis* (Amur maackia), from Manchuria and Siberia, is not as shapely as yellowwood but has creamy yellow flowers in late summer. Cold-hardy, useful in Zones 4 to 6, perhaps Zone 3.

CLERODENDRUM TRICHOTOMUM

clair-o-DEN-drum try-KOT-a-mum

Harlequin glorybower

Clerodendrum trichotomum

- **Fragrant small white flowers with reddish calyces, late summer**
- **Small bluish berries with persistent deep red calyces**
- **Zones 7 to 9, Zones 5 and 6 as cut-back shrub**

This 5- to 6-foot cut-back shrub (Zones 5 and 6), or tall shrub or tree 12 to 15 feet (Zones 7 to 9) from China and Japan, is moderately colorful in bloom but comes into its own as the dark metallic blue-green fruits ripen, attached to the red calyces. Its 6- to 8-inch leaves resemble those of catalpa.

USES: Screen, specimen, back of shrub border.

CULTURE: Grows well in any well-drained garden soil, preferably somewhat acidic even though dry. Flowers and fruits best in full sun.

RELATED SPECIES: *C. bungei* (Bunge glorybower or cashmere bouquet), a Chinese native, is lower growing than *C. trichotomum*, to 6 feet, with fragrant rosy-red flowers in 6- to 8-inch headlike clusters in summer. Like *C. trichotomum*, after freezing or pruning it returns vigorously and flowers the same year. Useful in Zones 8 to 10 and milder parts of Zone 7.

CLETHRA ALNIFOLIA

CLETH-ruh al-ni-FOL-ee-a

Summersweet

Clethra alnifolia *'Rosea'*

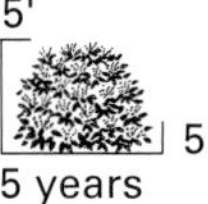

- **Fragrant flowers, midsummer**
- **Yellow to golden fall foliage, some years**
- **Tolerates wet soil**
- **Zones 5 to 9+, milder parts of Zone 4**

This 8- to 10-foot shrub spreads by suckers but is not difficult to control. It grows in wet soils in the wild in the eastern United States, and tolerates wet sites. In dry soils it is stressed and becomes susceptible to mites.

USES: Screen, back of a shrub border, or naturalizing.

CULTURE: Needs moist, at least slightly acidic soil (below pH 6.5) in full sun to half shade.

CULTIVARS: 'Creel's Calico' has white flowers and white-speckled foliage. Found in South Carolina, it is hardy in Zones 6 to 9+. 'Hummingbird' has white flowers and compact growth, less than 5 to 6 feet. 'Pink Spire' and 'Rosea' have pink flowers and become full-sized plants.

RELATED SPECIES: *C. barbinervis* (Japanese clethra) has more character as a specimen, growing 15 to 20 feet tall with a graceful habit, dark green foliage, pendulous 6-inch clusters of fragrant white flowers, and cinnamon-brown, shredding bark.

CORNUS FLORIDA

CORN-us FLOR-i-da

Flowering dogwood

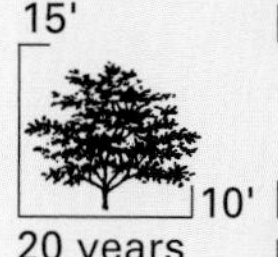
15'
10'
20 years

- **Showy flower bracts expand before leaves in mid- to late spring**
- **Horizontal branching**
- **Bright red fruits, autumn**
- **Maroon to crimson autumn foliage**
- **Slow-growing; interesting when young**
- **Zones 5 to 9**

Native to the eastern United States as far south as central Florida, this tree grows to 30 feet tall and wider. Its horizontal branching is especially appealing when accentuated by the flowers.

USES: Effective from a distance or at close range, as a patio tree, or in small groups.

CULTURE: Soil must be slightly acidic and perfectly drained for this tree. It can't be planted even an inch too deep. Fine in full sun where summers are cool, or in half shade. Anthracnose has killed many dogwoods in the East. Ideal conditions for young trees reduces stress. See also the C. *florida* × C. *kousa* hybrids, under C. *kousa*.

CULTIVARS: 'Cherokee Princess' and 'Cloud Nine' are superior clones with white bracts. 'Cherokee Chief' and 'Sweetwater' have pink to red bracts. 'Rainbow' and 'Welchii' have white bracts and tricolored leaves (white, pink, and green). 'Welchii Junior Miss' has pink bracts, white at the tips and bases; most important, it has a lesser chilling requirement for breaking dormancy so is better adapted to Zones 9 and 10.

RELATED SPECIES: C. *nuttallii* (Pacific dogwood), a native of the Pacific Northwest, grows to 75 feet tall, with six-bracted inflorescences, but does not do well far from its native habitat. It is susceptible to dogwood anthracnose.

Cornus florida *'Cloud Nine'*

Cornus florida *'Cherokee Chief'*

CORNUS KOUSA

CORN-us KOO-sa

Chinese or Japanese dogwood

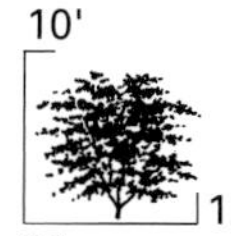
10'
12'
20 years

- **White flower bracts after leaves unfold in late spring and early summer**
- **Horizontal branching**
- **1-inch red fruits, late summer and fall**
- **Dull to bright red autumn foliage**
- **Slow-growing; interesting when young**
- **Zones 5 to 8**

This native of China, Japan, and Korea grows 15 to 20 feet tall and wider. Its horizontal branching, like that of flowering dogwood, is an asset. Blooming later, it complements flowering dogwood, and its pointed bracts form four-pointed stars against handsome green foliage.

USES: Much the same as for flowering dogwood.

CULTURE: Much the same as for flowering dogwood but more resistant to anthracnose.

VARIETY AND CULTIVARS: The variety *chinensis* is thought to be superior in flower, based on a limited representation of trees. 'China Girl' is free-flowering, even as a young tree. 'Gold Star' has strikingly variegated leaves with golden centers and green margins. 'Milky Way', selected from var. *chinensis*, is free-flowering with good form and heavy fruiting. 'Lustgarten Weeping' and 'Pendula' have strongly weeping habits. 'Summer Stars' has abundant small flowers that hold their bracts for many weeks.

HYBRIDS: C. × *rutgersensis* (Rutgers hybrids), between C. *florida* and C. *kousa*, are resistant to both dogwood borers and anthracnose; they flower in late spring. Specific cultivars are 'Rutban' (Aurora™), 'Rutcan' (Constellation™), 'Rutdan' ('Galaxy'), and 'Rutlan' (Ruth Ellen™), all with white bracts; 'Rutgan' (Stellar Pink™), has pink bracts.

Cornus kousa

Cornus kousa

CORNUS MAS

CORN-*us* MAS

Cornelian cherry

Cornus mas

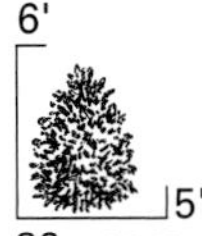

- **Profusion of small yellow flowers, early spring**
- **Cherrylike red fruits, summer**
- **Lustrous dark green leaves**
- **Zones 5 to 8**

This native of southeastern Europe and western Asia grows 15 to 18 feet tall and wide, with a broad oval shape.

USES: Its fullness and foliage make it a prime screening shrub or hedge. It can also be trained as a small tree, and its mist of small yellow flowers is especially effective against a dark background.

CULTURE: It grows well in any good garden soil but does not tolerate wet soils as well as other shrub dogwoods. It grows well in full sun or partial shade and fairly well, although less compactly, in full shade.

CULTIVARS: 'Golden Glory' blooms profusely and is narrower in outline.

RELATED SPECIES: *C. officinalis* (Japanese cornel), the Asian counterpart of Cornelian cherry, is similar in size and flowering but more open and picturesque in habit. It is better suited for use as a patio tree but less suited for screening.

CORYLOPSIS PAUCIFLORA

cor-i-LOP-sis paw-si-FLOR-a

Buttercup winter hazel

Corylopsis pauciflora

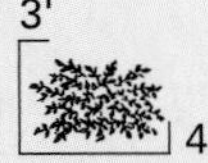

- **Fragrant yellow flowers in midspring**
- **Slender zigzag stems, horizontal branching**
- **Bluish-green leaves turn yellow in autumn some years**
- **Zones 6 to 8**

This graceful shrub in the witch-hazel family *(Hamamelidaceae)* usually grows less than 6 feet tall and spreads to 8 feet wide. Its pale yellow flowers, in drooping clusters to nearly 2 inches long, are especially effective in midspring against a dark background, and its foliage turns clear yellow in autumn in some years.

USES: It is graceful as a specimen for accent, in a shrub border, or naturalized on woodland edges.

CULTURE: Best in well-drained, somewhat acidic soils (below pH 6.0) in full sun or half shade.

RELATED SPECIES: *C. glabrescens* (fragrant winter hazel) is a larger shrub, 10 to 12 feet tall and broader, with brighter yellow flowers. It is slightly more cold-hardy, to parts of Zone 5. *C. sinensis* (Chinese winter hazel) is similar to fragrant winter hazel but with slightly larger leaves and flower clusters. *C. spicata* (spike winter hazel) is similar in size to buttercup winter hazel but with brighter yellow flowers.

COTINUS COGGYGRIA

co-TY-nus co-JIG-ree-a

Smoketree

Cotinus coggygria *'Royal Purple'*

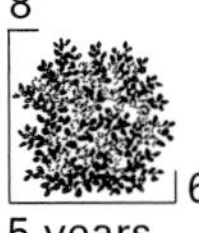

- **Cloudlike or "smoky" inflorescences early to late summer**
- **Rounded shrub 10 to 12 feet, interesting foliage**
- **Orange, red, or purple autumn foliage**
- **Zones 5 to 7**

The "smoke" of this shrub is neither its flowers nor fruits but the multiple stalks on which they are borne, persisting as masses resembling cotton candy. In the species the "smoke" is pale yellow-green, and the blue-green foliage turns gold to orange in autumn.

USES: Specimen for accent, part of a shrub border, or massed for large-scale effect.

CULTURE: Does well in any well-drained or even dry soil in full sun or light shade. Heavy spring pruning forces vigorous and more colorful shoots and produces maximum leaf color in the red and purple cultivars (but at the expense of flowers and "smoke").

CULTIVARS: 'Nordine' has rosy purplish foliage, turning yellow-orange in autumn, and rosy pink "smoke." 'Royal Purple' has deep purple foliage, turning red-purple in autumn, and red-purple "smoke." 'Velvet Cloak' has bright rosy purple foliage, turning wine red in autumn, and rosy-red "smoke."

COTONEASTER SPECIES

co-TOE-nee-aster

Cotoneaster

- White or pink flowers in mid- to late spring
- Lustrous deciduous or evergreen leaves
- Red fruits
- Spreading growth habit

These variable and versatile plants, mostly from Asia, are both beautiful and functional.
USES: Ground cover (with mulch), rock garden, shrub border, specimen, or screen.
CULTURE: These plants perform well in just about any well-drained garden soil, in full sun for best fruiting. They are susceptible to a variety of insects and diseases. The species listed are not usually affected seriously except in the South (especially mites and scale insects) and in northern areas where fire blight is common.
SPECIES AND CULTIVARS:

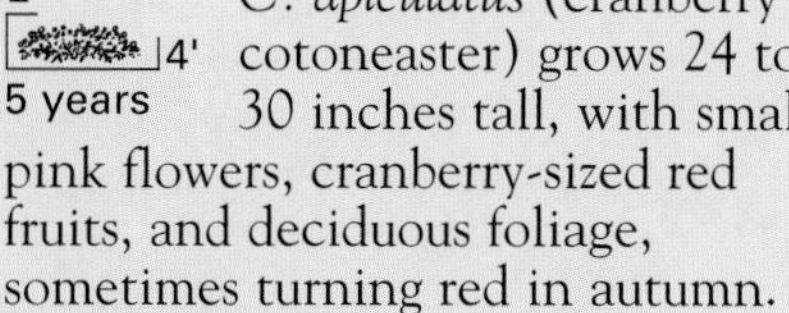

2' 4' 5 years

C. apiculatus (cranberry cotoneaster) grows 24 to 30 inches tall, with small pink flowers, cranberry-sized red fruits, and deciduous foliage, sometimes turning red in autumn. Hardy in Zones 5 to 8 and very popular in the Midwest and Northeast.

1' 6' 5 years

C. dammeri (bearberry cotoneaster) has small white flowers, handsome semievergreen to evergreen foliage, long-lasting red berries, and rapid, low-spreading growth, hardy in Zones 6 to 9. 'Coral Beauty' is full-fruiting, hardy to parts of Zone 5.

1' 4' 5 years

C. horizontalis (rockspray cotoneaster) is similar in height and flowering to cranberry cotoneaster but slightly less cold-hardy, with smaller, lustrous fruits and distinctive fish-bone branching.

5' 4' 5 years

C. salicifolius (willowleaf cotoneaster) grows 8 to 10 feet tall in time, with a gracefully arching habit, handsome 3-inch leathery evergreen to semievergreen leaves, small white flowers, and red fruits in profusion in autumn and early winter. Hardy in Zones 6 to 9.

Cotoneaster salicifolius

CRATAEGUS CRUS-GALLI

cruh-TEE-gus crus-GAHL-ee

Cockspur hawthorn

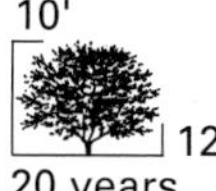

10' 12' 20 years

- Quantities of white flowers, late spring
- Strong horizontal branching, slow growth
- Glossy dark green leaves and very large thorns
- Bright red fruits persist into fall
- Zones 4 to 7

This tree, to 25 feet tall and wider in time, is showy in flower, accentuating its horizontal branching. Its ½-inch red fruits are also showy if not covered with cedar-apple rust pustules. Its superb foliage is less likely to be affected.
USES: Specimen tree or large-scale massing.
CULTURE: Thrives in any well-drained soil; best in full sun.
CULTIVAR: 'Inermis' is a thornless selection valued for its safety.
RELATED SPECIES: *C. laevigata* (English hawthorn or May tree) is one of the showiest of the hawthorns, with white, pink, or red flowers followed by bright red fruits, which persist into early autumn. It is less cold-hardy than the other hawthorns listed here (Zones 6 to 9), and more subject to problems except on the West Coast, where it is better adapted. Cultivars include 'Paulii', with double crimson flowers, and 'Crimson Cloud', with single red and white flowers.

C. phaenopyrum (Washington hawthorn), growing to 20 feet tall, seldom shows signs of rust. It flowers a week or so after cockspur hawthorn, its small, glossy red fruits making a major show well into winter. Its foliage also often turns red in autumn.

C. viridis (green hawthorn) 'Winter King' is a popular hawthorn, growing to 25 feet tall, with early white flowers, silvery bark, and nonglossy orange-red fruits that persist through December.

Crataegus crus-galli

Crataegus phaenopyrum

CYTISUS X PRAECOX

SIT-i-sus × PREE-cox

Warminster broom

Cytisus × praecox

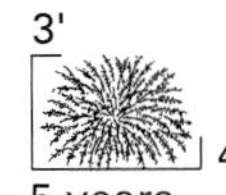

- **Pealike pale yellow flowers, midspring**
- **Slender green stems appear broomlike**
- **Zones 6 to 9**

This shrub, 4 to 5 feet tall, is remarkably showy in bloom, and its green stems provide interest year-round.

USES: Rock garden, shrub border, or alone for accent.

CULTURE: Needs perfect soil drainage and full sun.

CULTIVARS: 'Albus' grows to 3 feet, with white flowers. 'Allgold' has golden-yellow flowers. 'Hollandia' has pink and red flowers. 'Zeelandia' is fast-growing, with pale yellow, cream, and lilac-pink flowers.

RELATED SPECIES: *C. decumbens* (prostrate broom) is an excellent foot-high ground cover with bright golden-yellow flowers in late spring. *C. scoparius* (Scotch broom) grows wild in central and southern Europe, to 6 feet tall, with larger flowers. 'Andreanus' has yellow and deep red flowers. 'Burkwoodii' has reddish-brown flowers. 'Golden Sunlight' is a spreader, with bright yellow flowers. 'Moonlight' is upright, with pale yellow flowers. 'Pink Beauty' has pink flowers. 'Red Wings' and 'San Francisco' have deep red flowers.

DAPHNE X BURKWOODII

DAF-nee burk-WOOD-ee-eye

Burkwood daphne

Daphne × burkwoodii *'Briggs Moonlight'*

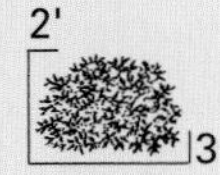

- **Small, fragrant white flowers, pink in bud, midspring**
- **Small blue-green evergreen or semievergreen leaves**
- **Zones 5 to 7**

This hybrid of Eurasian species grows 3 to 5 feet tall and wide, with fragrant flowers. Fruits and foliage of some daphnes have proved to be toxic, and it is safe to assume that others are also.

USES: Rock garden, specimen, front of shrub border, massing.

CULTURE: Perfect soil drainage is essential; a few hours of flooding can be lethal. Heavy soils can be lightened with sand and small amounts of organic matter. Container-grown plants have better transplanting success. Tolerates full sun or considerable shade.

CULTIVARS: 'Carol Mackie' has dark green leaves edged in pale yellow. 'Briggs Moonlight' has the colors reversed (the edging is green) and is slower-growing.

RELATED SPECIES: *D. cneorum* (rose daphne) grows less than a foot in height, with small, more-or-less evergreen leaves and delightfully fragrant rose-pink flowers. It needs perfectly drained soil, preferably sandy. 'Alba' has white flowers, and 'Ruby Glow' is a fine rose-pink selection.

DAPHNE ODORA

DAF-nee o-DOR-a

Winter daphne

Daphne odora *'Aureomarginata'*

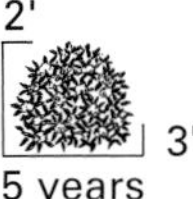

- **Small, very fragrant rosy purple or white flowers, early to midspring**
- **Lustrous evergreen leaves, 2 to 3 inches long**
- **Zones 7 to 9+**

This compact evergreen shrub from China grows 3 to 5 feet tall and wide in time. Foliage and fruits of all daphnes are probably toxic (see *D. × burkwoodii*).

USES: Same as Burkwood daphne but fully evergreen.

CULTURE: Needs perfectly drained soil with no possibility of flooding. Container-grown plants have better transplanting success. Best in half to full shade.

CULTIVARS: 'Alba' has ivory-white flowers. 'Aureomarginata' has light yellow-margined leaves and rosy purple flowers, nearly white inside, and is slightly more cold-hardy than the species.

RELATED SPECIES: *D. mezereum* (February daphne), from Europe and western Asia, is naturalized in northeastern North America. It is deciduous, growing to 4 feet tall but narrower. Its rosy purple flowers, which appear before the leaves, are showy. Its small, poisonous bright scarlet fruits are borne close to the stems in late summer. 'Album' has white flowers and yellow fruits.

DAVIDIA INVOLUCRATA

duh-VID-ee-a in-vol-yew-CRAY-ta

Dove tree

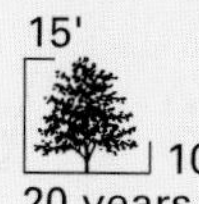

- Showy white bracts in late spring
- Coarsely toothed bright green leaves
- Subdued orange-pink inner bark adds color in winter
- Zones 6 to 8

This tree was the reason for the young E. H. "Chinese" Wilson's first plant exploration to China, on behalf of the Messrs. Veitch nursery in England. Wilson went on to become one of the most famous plant explorers of the 20th century. Each globose yellow flower cluster of this tree is held between two papery white bracts, the lower one 6 inches long, the upper half that length, giving the effect of a white dove perched in the tree, a striking sight when there are hundreds in a tree. Flowering seldom occurs two years running, so the sight is greatly anticipated. The tree itself is pyramidal when young and grows to 40 or more feet tall.

USES: Lawn shade tree, patio tree, or accent in a shrub border.

CULTURE: Grows best in good, well-drained garden soil, at least slightly acidic (below pH 6.5), and in full sun to light shade.

VARIETY: The variety *vilmoriniana* has slightly duller, smoother foliage and may be slightly more cold-hardy.

Davidia involucrata

DEUTZIA GRACILIS

DEWT-see-a gra-SIL-iss

Slender deutzia

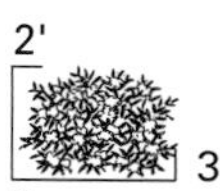

- Showy white flowers in upright clusters, late spring
- Moundlike habit, to 3 feet
- Zones 5 to 8

This low plant from Japan is valued for its flowering and small size.

USES: Low informal hedge, or the front of the shrub border.

CULTURE: Needs renewal pruning every few years. Does well in almost any well-drained soil, and flowers best in full sun or light shade.

RELATED SPECIES AND HYBRIDS: *Deutzia crenata* 'Nikko' (Nikko deutzia) has also been listed as a cultivar of slender deutzia. It grows to 2 feet tall, with small, double white flowers and small leaves that turn dull purple in autumn. *D.* × *lemoinei* (Lemoine deutzia), a hybrid of slender deutzia, functions as a larger edition of that species, growing 6 to 8 feet tall. *D.* × *lemoinei* 'Compactum' is similar but more compact, reaching only 5 feet. *D. scabra* (fuzzy deutzia) is a larger shrub, to at least 8 feet, with clusters of white flowers, blushed purplish pink on the outsides. A superior selection of *D. scabra*, 'Codsall Pink', has double pink flowers and orange-brown bark.

Deutzia × hybrida *'Mont Rose'*

ENKIANTHUS CAMPANULATUS

en-kee-ANN-thus cam-PAN-you-LAY-tus

Redvein enkianthus

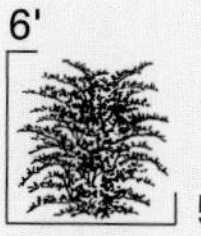

- Bell-shaped flowers, mid- to late spring
- Upright deciduous shrub
- Interesting tiered branching
- Red autumn foliage
- Zones 5 to 8

This Japanese member of the heath family *(Ericaceae)* grows 10 to 12 feet tall and 8 to 10 feet wide in time. Its ½-inch flowers—pink-lined yellow, or red—provide spring color; its fall foliage color is more intense.

USE: Massed, or in a border with other acid-loving plants.

CULTURE: Needs well-drained soil, not as acidic as some other acid-loving plants but below pH 6.0.

CULTIVARS: 'Albiflorus' has whitish flowers. 'Hollandia Red' has unusually showy deep pink to red flowers. 'Red Bells' has stronger red veining in the flowers and outstanding red fall foliage. 'Red Velvet' has deep pink flowers.

RELATED SPECIES: *E. perulatus* (white enkianthus) is more compact, about 6 feet tall and wide, with small white flowers and bright green leaves, turning yellow-orange in autumn.

Enkianthus campanulatus

ERICA CARNEA

AIR-i-ka CAR-nee-a

Spring heath

Erica carnea *'Foxhollow Mahogany'*

5 years

- **Red, pink, or white flowers, early spring**
- **Evergreen ground cover**
- **Needs well-drained, acidic soil**
- **Varied foliage colors**
- **Zones 6 and 7, Zone 5 with reliable snow cover**

Spring heath is similar to Scotch heather *(Calluna vulgaris)* in function, flower and foliage colors, and site requirements, but it flowers in late winter and early spring.

USES: Same as Scotch heather.

CULTURE: Same as Scotch heather (see page 39).

CULTIVARS: Many are available. 'Aurea' has golden foliage in direct sun. 'King George' and 'Vivellii' have bright rosy red flowers. 'Pink Spangles' has pink and lilac flowers and dark green foliage. 'Springwood Pink' has rose-pink flowers and bronzed new foliage. 'Winter Beauty' has dark lilac-pink flowers and deep green leaves. 'Springwood White' has white flowers and dark green foliage but is otherwise like 'Springwood Pink'.

RELATED SPECIES: Darley heath *(E. × darleyensis)* is hardy in Zones 7 and 8, and grows 10 to 18 inches tall. *E. tetralix* (cross-leaved heath) is hardy in Zones 5 to 7, Zone 4 with reliable snow cover.

ERYTHRINA CRISTA-GALLI

air-i-THRY-na KRIST-a-GAHL-ee

Cockspur coral tree

Erythrina crista-galli

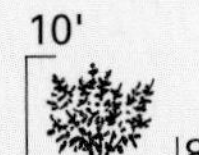

20 years

- **Bright red flowers, spring to fall**
- **Shrub or small tree**
- **Strong spines on stems, petioles, and leaf midribs**
- **Zones 9 to 10+**

After the leaves of this deciduous tree from Brazil have unfolded, the crimson flowers open in as many as three flushes from spring to autumn. The flowering branches die back after flowering. The tree may be frost-killed to the ground in Zone 9 but will grow back in spring, persisting as a shrub. In Zone 10, it may reach 15 to 20 feet tall.

USES: Specimen for color where the spines are not a problem. Its large leaves make it an effective shade tree in Zone 10+.

CULTURE: Should be pruned to remove the spent flowering branches, and after freezes to remove the winter-killed top. Best in full sun.

RELATED SPECIES: *E. humeana* (Natal coral tree) 'Raja' is usually trained to about 10 feet tall and 8 feet wide for floral display. Its orange-red flowers are borne in 18-inch clusters from late summer through autumn. The trunk and leaf undersides are spiny.

ESCALLONIA X EXONIENSIS

ESS-ka-LONE-ee-a ex-on-ee-EN-sis

Escallonia

Escallonia × langleyensis *'Apple Blossom'*

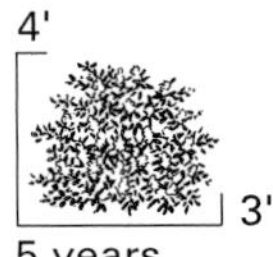

5 years

- **White, pink, or red flowers, summer and fall**
- **Fast-growing evergreen shrub to 10 feet tall**
- **Small, glossy leaves**
- **Zones 8 to 10**

The parent species of this hybrid group—*E. rosea* and *E. rubra*—like most other escallonia species, are native to Chile. They are valued for their small, glossy leaves and clusters of flowers in summer and fall in Zones 8 and 9. In Zone 10, they flower nearly year-round.

USES: Screening, massing, shrub border, or as a windbreak in Zones 9 and 10.

CULTURE: Easily grown where adapted, except in alkaline soils (above pH 7.5). Responds well to pruning, after flowers fade, for renewal or to reduce its size. Can be sheared as a formal hedge, at the expense of some bloom. Best in full sun, and very tolerant of wind.

CULTIVARS: 'Frades' (Pink Princess™) has rose-pink flowers and grows to only 6 feet tall.

RELATED SPECIES AND HYBRIDS: *E. × langleyensis* (hybrid between *E. rubra* and *E. virgata)* 'Apple Blossom' grows to 5 feet tall and wide with pruning to maintain its form. Another hybrid, 'Red Elf', is compact, with red flowers.

EUCALYPTUS SPECIES

you-kuh-LIP-tus

Eucalyptus, Gum

- Showy flowers in some species
- Mostly fast-growing tall trees
- Handsome bark, often bicolored
- Greenish-to-silver-blue evergreen leaves
- Adaptable, low-maintenance trees
- Zones 9 and 10 (in the West)

These distinctive trees from Australia are popular in the warm Southwest. Some 20 species are available in this country as plants, nearly 200 more as seeds. Relatively few have showy flowers.

USES: Fast-growing shade trees, screens, or windbreaks.

CULTURE: Most are difficult to transplant. Young bare-root seedlings do best (if potted they must not be pot-bound). They tolerate dry soil once established but need water at transplanting and occasionally until they are growing strongly. They need full sun for success.

SPECIES: Here are some of the best for showy flowers.

40' 20' 20 years

E. calophylla (Marri eucalyptus) is a medium to large round-headed tree to 50 feet tall in California. It has outstanding broad-oval leaves, and showy white, pink, or red flowers in 1-foot clusters, intermittently through the year. Useful in Zone 10+.

20' 20' 20 years

E. erythrocorys (red cap gum) is a small tree to 25 feet tall. Bright red caps cover the inflorescence, then drop off to show the yellow flower clusters, at different times, mostly in winter. Best trained as a shrub or multiple-trunked tree. Tolerates irrigation if soil is very well-drained. Zone 10+.

Eucalyptus erythrocorys

Eucalyptus ficifolia

25' 10' 20 years

E. ficifolia (red-flowering gum) is a round-headed tree to 35 feet with a compact crown, or it can be treated as a large shrub. Flowers are light red or sometimes orange, pink, or creamy white, in showy 1-foot clusters. Mildest Zone 10+.

E. gunnii (cider gum) is a dense, vertical tree from 40 to 80 feet, with small creamy yellow flowers in early summer. Strong and vigorous, it makes a good shade tree or windbreak in Zones 9 to 10+ and much of Zone 8.

30' 20' 20 years

E. leucoxylon (white ironbark) is a variable, slender, upright tree, 20 to 40 feet tall, with weeping branch tips and 6-inch sickle-shaped gray-green leaves. Small clusters of creamy white flowers open intermittently in winter and spring. Zones 9 to 10+. The selection 'Rosea' is more shrubby, with crimson flowers.

E. pauciflora ssp. *niphophila* (snow gum) is a small, open tree to 20 feet tall, with silvery blue lanceolate foliage, smooth white bark, and creamy white flowers in small clusters in summer. Zones 8 to 10+.

E. preissiana (bell-fruited mallee) is an open, multi-trunked shrub (mallee) to 12 feet, or a single-trunked tree to 15 feet. It has dull blue leaves on red stems, and showy yellow flowers from middle to late winter. Useful in Zone 10+.

Eucalyptus preissiana

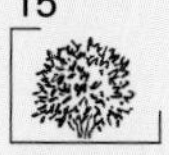

E. pyriformis (pearpod mallee) is a mallee with slender, rangy 10- to 15-foot stems. Showy 3-inch red, pink, orange, yellow, or cream flowers in clusters, from late winter to early summer, are followed by 1-inch pear-shaped fruits. Useful in Zone 10+; best in dry, sandy soil.

E. robusta (swamp mahogany) is a tall tree (to 75 feet) with dense foliage, eventually round-headed, with lustrous dark green leaves. Masses of pink-tinted creamy white flowers open intermittently during the year, mostly in winter. Useful in Zones 9 to 10+ and mildest Zone 8; tolerates moist or saline soil.

E. torquata (coral gum) is a narrowly upright tree to 15 feet tall, with coral and yellow flowers in repeated flushes during the year. Seed capsules may be removed to reduce weight on the plant and preserve its form. Zones 10+.

Eucalyptus torquata

EXOCHORDA X MACRANTHA

ex-o-KOR-da ma-CRAN-tha

Hybrid pearlbush

Exochorda × macrantha *'The Bride'*

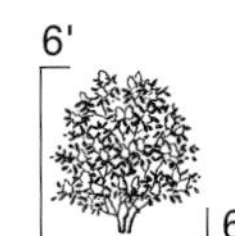

- **Masses of white flowers, midspring**
- **Well-shaped shrub to 10 feet tall in time**
- **Zones 6 to 8, milder parts of Zone 5**

This showy hybrid of a Chinese species has dull green foliage. After flowering, it reverts to its role as a background plant for the rest of the year. It is called pearlbush because the spherical flower buds appear as white pearls before they open.

USES: Screen, or background for smaller, more colorful shrubs in summer.

CULTURE: Does well in any good garden soil in full sun or light shade. Needs little care other than renewal pruning every few years.

CULTIVAR: 'The Bride' is a low-growing selection, 4 to 5 feet tall and much wider. It becomes a solid mass of white flowers in spring.

RELATED SPECIES: *E. giraldii* var. *wilsonii* (Wilson pearlbush), from northwest China, was introduced by E. H. "Chinese" Wilson, who brought it to North America. It has some of the largest flowers of this group. *E. racemosa* (common pearlbush), from eastern China, has slightly smaller flowers. It is the hardiest of the group, to Zone 5.

FORSYTHIA X INTERMEDIA

for-SYTHE-ee-a in-ter-MEE-dee-a

Border forsythia

Forsythia × intermedia *'Lynwood'*

Forsythia suspensa

- **Brilliant pale to deep golden-yellow flowers before leaves emerge in early to middle spring**
- **Graceful moundlike shrub with arching branches to 8 feet tall and wider**
- **Lustrous medium green leaves**
- **Zones 5 to 8**

This shrub's flowers are a bold sign of spring, but its flower buds are winter-killed at -15 degrees to -18 degrees F, so it does not flower reliably in Zone 5. Its habit is part of its charm.

USES: Specimen or in a shrub border.

CULTURE: Does well in any good garden soil in full sun or moderate shade. Needs renewal pruning every few years. Shearing it as a hedge would eliminate its graceful habit and most of its flowers.

CULTIVARS: 'Lynwood', 'Spectabilis', and 'Spring Glory' are superior clones. 'Courtasol' (Gold Tide™) is low-growing, to 2 feet.

RELATED SPECIES AND HYBRIDS: *F. suspensa* (weeping forsythia), the Japanese parent of border forsythia, is pendulous in habit, making it ideal for planting at the top of a retaining wall so its flowering branches cascade down. Its var. *sieboldii* is even more strongly pendulous in habit. The var. *fortunei* is not often seen, but strongly resembles border forsythia.

F. viridissima (greenstem forsythia), from China, is notable for the dwarf selection 'Bronxensis', which makes an effective ground cover but flowers only weakly.

F. ovata (Korean forsythia) is more stiffly upright and a little earlier to flower, with somewhat more cold-hardy flower buds, to about -20 degrees F (Zones 5 to 8 and parts of Zone 4). It is the parent of several hardier selections. 'New Hampshire Gold', a hybrid with 'Lynwood', has flower buds hardy to about -23 degrees F. Hybrids with the Albanian *F. europaea* (European forsythia), including 'Meadowlark' and 'Northern Gold', are remarkably hardy, with flower buds that withstand -40 degrees F and lower in winter, making them hardy as far north as North Dakota (Zones 4 to 7 and perhaps parts of Zone 3).

Abeliophyllum distichum (Korean abelialeaf, sometimes called white forsythia) is a close relative of *Forsythia*. Its smaller, sometimes pink-tinted white flowers appear with the earliest forsythias in early spring, and its flower buds are at least as hardy as those of Korean forsythia. Its deep green, lustrous foliage is handsome in summer. Hardy in Zones 5 to 9.

FOTHERGILLA MAJOR

faw-ther-GIL-a MAY-jer

Large fothergilla

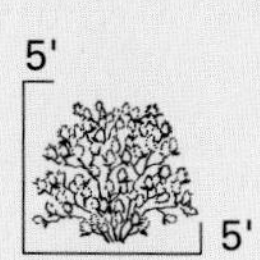

- **Fragrant creamy-white flowers, midspring**
- **Outstanding red to gold autumn foliage**
- **Trouble-free native shrub**
- **Zones 5 to 8**

This native of southern Appalachia grows 8 to 10 feet tall and nearly as wide. It and its smaller relative, below, are among the very finest plants for fall foliage color.

USES: Specimen, screen, massing, or naturalizing in open woodland.

CULTURE: This plant in the witch hazel family *(Hamamelidaceae)* is best dug and transplanted as new growth is just beginning. Plants dug fully dormant have little root activity and may fail. This is less important when container-grown plants are used. Once established, it grows well in average to moist garden soil in full sun or half shade and seldom needs pruning or much other care.

RELATED SPECIES: *F. gardenii* (dwarf fothergilla), native to the southeastern coastal plain, is smaller than large fothergilla, growing 4 to 6 feet tall in time. Flower clusters and leaves are also smaller, but autumn foliage is similar.

Fothergilla major

FRANKLINIA ALATAMAHA

frank-LIN-ee-a a-lay-ta-MAY-ha

Franklin tree

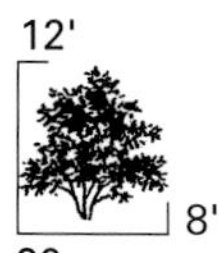

- **Showy white flowers, late summer and autumn**
- **Lustrous dark green leaves turn wine red in autumn**
- **Striped light gray bark**
- **Zones 6 to 8, Zone 9 and 10 (in the West)**

This small tree or shrub in the camellia family *(Theaceae)* grows 10 to 15 feet tall and nearly as wide, with leathery leaves followed by 3-inch flowers which look like single camellias, from late summer until frost. Discovered in Georgia by early Philadelphia nurseryman John Bartram and named for Benjamin Franklin, it is now believed extinct in the wild.

USES: Specimen tree, for its unique interest.

CULTURE: Best in well-drained soil that is somewhat acidic (below pH 6.0). This plant is susceptible to *Phytophthora* wilt disease (root rot). As with rhododendrons and dogwoods, it needs the best possible environment and should not be planted too deeply. If *Phytophthora* is diagnosed, this tree should not be replanted in the same place. Needs full sun to half shade in the North; some shade in the South. On the West Coast, may need irrigation.

Franklinia alatamaha

FUCHSIA HYBRIDS

FEW-sha

Fuchsia

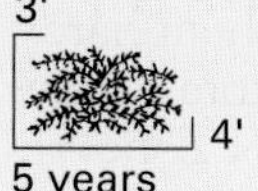

- **Pendulous red, pink, or purple flowers, mostly in summer**
- **Lustrous green foliage, red-marked in some cultivars**
- **Shrubby to cascading habit**
- **Zones 9 and 10 (in the West)**

These colorful hybrids of *F. fulgens*, from Mexico, and *F. magellanica*, from Peru and Chile, are at their best on the West Coast, where they grow rapidly to 3 feet tall and wider, with gracefully arching branches Their 2-inch flowers, resembling hanging lanterns, have crimson sepals surrounding purple, pink, or white petals.

USES: Specimen, border, or container shrub in colder climates.

CULTURE: Plant in rich, moist, well-drained soil in full sun to half shade in cool summers, more shade in hot summers. Appreciates misting when humidity is low.

CULTIVARS: Many exist; select for habit, color, and local availability.

RELATED SPECIES: *F. magellanica* (Magellan fuchsia) is the most cold-hardy species, to Zone 8 and the mildest parts of Zone 7. It is a shrub to 4 feet tall and broader, with smaller lanternlike flowers.

Fuchsia magellanica

GARDENIA AUGUSTA (FORMERLY G. JASMINOIDES)

gar-DEE-nee-a aw-GUS-ta

Gardenia

Gardenia augusta

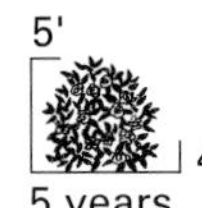

- **Large waxy white flowers in summer are extremely fragrant**
- **Large evergreen leaves**
- **Zones 9 and 10, milder parts of Zone 8**

This shrub, 4 to 6 feet tall and nearly as wide, is attractive for its glossy, prominently veined leaves, 4 to 6 inches long. But it really comes into its own in early summer, when the 3- to 4-inch creamy white single, or more often double, flowers begin to open, releasing their strong, sweet fragrance.
USES: Specimen or shrub border, for fragrance. If massed, the fragrance may be overwhelming.
CULTURE: Needs well-drained but moist, acidic soil and semishade where summers are hot. Tolerates full sun in mild coastal climates but requires some heat for flowering, so it does not perform well along the Pacific coast north of California.
CULTIVARS: 'August Beauty' has long-lasting flowers all summer. 'Mystery' flowers in early summer. 'Radicans' (dwarf gardenia) grows only 1 to 2 feet tall, with many small flowers, and is a good ground cover. 'Radicans Variegata' is similar but has white-margined leaves. 'Veitchii' is compact, with double flowers all summer.

GENISTA AETNENSIS

jen-ISS-ta et-NEN-sis

Mt. Etna broom

Genista aetnensis

- **Yellow flowers, late spring and early summer**
- **Graceful, open, leafless habit**
- **Broomlike green stems**
- **Zones 8 to 9+**

This small tree from Mt. Etna, Sicily, eventually grows 15 feet tall, with bright yellow flowers in midsummer on leafless green stems.
USES: Specimen for seasonal accent, or in a shrub border.
CULTURE: Thrives in well-drained soil in full sun or light shade.
RELATED SPECIES AND CULTIVARS: G. *pilosa* (silkleaf woadwaxen) 'Vancouver Gold' is prostrate, about 1 foot high, with silky twigs. Its flowers make a solid mat of gold in spring; excellent in a rock garden or as a ground cover for full sun and well-drained soil in Zones 6 to 8. G. *sagittalis* (winged broom) is a hardy ground cover in Zones 3 to 7, with yellow flowers in early summer. Its broadly winged stems give the appearance of an evergreen. G. *tinctoria* (Dyer's greenwood) is a low shrub with small semievergreen leaves and yellow flowers opening in early summer, useful in Zones 3 to 7. 'Plena' grows 16 inches tall, with double flowers. 'Royal Gold' grows 2 feet tall, with many flowers.

HALESIA TETRAPTERA (FORMERLY H. CAROLINA)

HALE-zee-a tet-RAP-ter-a

Carolina silverbell

Halesia tetraptera *'Rosea'*

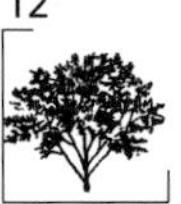

- **Clusters of bell-shaped white flowers, late spring**
- **Pendulous 4-winged fruits**
- **Smooth, subtly striped bark on young trees, blocky on old ones**
- **Zones 5 to 8 (with attention to seed source)**

This tree is native from West Virginia to Florida and Texas, growing moderately slowly to 20 to 30 feet tall and valued for its flowers and small size. In the North, northernmost seed sources should be used.
USES: Shade or patio tree, or for naturalizing.
CULTURE: Grows best in well-drained, reasonably fertile, slightly acidic (below pH 6.0) garden soil. Pruning is seldom necessary. Best in full sun to light shade.
RELATED SPECIES: *H. monticola* (mountain silverbell), native to the southern Appalachians, is similar to Carolina silverbell except for its size. It grows 40 to 60 feet tall and wide in time, with slightly larger flowers and fruits. It is more cold-hardy than southern seed sources of Carolina silverbell. The selection 'Rosea' has light pink flowers.

HAMAMELIS X INTERMEDIA

ham-a-MEAL-is inter-MEE-dee-a

Hybrid witch hazel

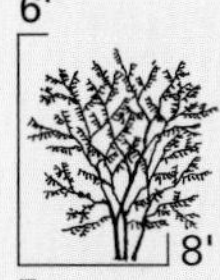

- **Yellow, orange, or red flowers, late winter or early spring**
- **Yellow, orange, or red fall foliage**
- **Flowers have spicy fragrance**
- **Zones 6 to 8**

These large shrubs are valued for their late-winter flowers.

USES: Specimen for color accent, or in the shrub border.
CULTURE: Plant in any well-drained garden soil in full sun for heaviest flowering. Even in considerable shade, there will be substantial flowering.
CULTIVARS: 'Arnold Promise' has showy yellow flowers. 'Diane' has deep red flowers, striking in good light. 'Jelena' has coppery orange flowers that glow on dark days or against a dark background.
RELATED SPECIES: *H. mollis* (Chinese witch hazel) and *H. japonica* (Japanese witch hazel) are the parents of *H.* × *intermedia*. Both are colorful on their own. Japanese witch hazel is a source of autumn foliage color. *H. virginiana* (common witch hazel), native to the eastern and central United States, is admired for its yellow flowers in autumn, colorful after leaf drop.

Hamamelis × intermedia *'Jelena'*

HEBE SPECIES

HEE-bee

Shrubby veronica

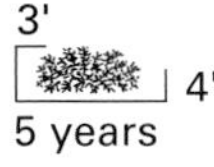

- **Showy flowers, summer**
- **Dark green to light blue evergreen foliage**
- **Zones 9 and 10**

These veronica relatives from New Zealand include creepers growing less than 1 foot tall and shrubs as tall as 5 to 6 feet. Most have showy flowers in summer, and all have evergreen foliage.

USES: Ground covers, rock garden specimens, hedges, and border shrubs. Effective in seaside plantings.
CULTURE: Plant in well-drained soil, better dry than wet, in full sun.
RELATED SPECIES: *H.* × *andersonii* (Anderson hebe), a hybrid of *H. speciosa* (showy hebe) and *H. salicifolia* (willowleaf hebe), grows compactly to 5 to 6 feet tall and wide, with fleshy deep green leaves and 2- to 4-inch spikes of white flowers, purple at the tip. *H. buxifolia* (boxleaf hebe) is a rounded, compact shrub to 5 feet, with small green leaves and small white flowers in headlike clusters. It is one of the hardier hebes. 'Patty's Purple' is a selection from *H. buxifolia,* with blue-purple flowers.

Hebe *'Patty's Purple'*

HEPTACODIUM MICONIOIDES

hep-ta-CODE-ee-um my-con-ee-oh-EYE-dees

Seven-son flower

- **Small creamy white flowers in late summer, followed by showy long-lasting red sepals**
- **Large shrub or small tree, to about 20 feet tall**
- **Handsome three-veined leaves**
- **Zones 6 to 9, probably also Zone 5**

E. H. Wilson brought specimens of this tall shrub to the United States from China in 1907, but live plants were not introduced until the 1980 Sino-American Botanical Expedition brought back viable seeds. The resulting plants grew very rapidly, with arching branches bearing handsome foliage and, later, quantities of white flowers. The main color is in the showy red sepals that remain after flowering, from late summer through fall. It is leggy, but its base can be hidden by smaller plants, or left to display the multiple trunks with peeling tan bark.

USES: Can be trained as an understory tree or planted as a specimen in a shrub border.
CULTURE: Needs well-drained garden soil. Does well in full sun or considerable shade. Pruning back leading shoots promotes fullness.

Above: Heptacodium miconioides in bloom. Inset: colorful sepals.

HIBISCUS SYRIACUS

hi-BISS-kus seer-ee-AY-kus

Rose of Sharon

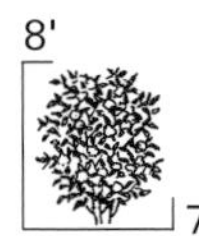

- **Large flowers, late summer**
- **Lobed bright green leaves, sparsely arranged**
- **Upright, open habit**
- **Zones 5 to 9**

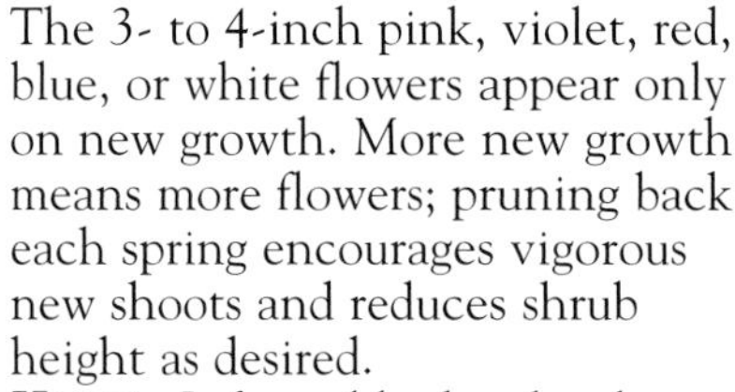

The 3- to 4-inch pink, violet, red, blue, or white flowers appear only on new growth. More new growth means more flowers; pruning back each spring encourages vigorous new shoots and reduces shrub height as desired.

USES: Informal hedge, border shrub, or very small tree, for late summer color.

CULTURE: Needs well-drained garden soil. Appreciates water and light fertilizer at pruning time.

CULTIVARS: 'Ardens' has double blue-tinted purple flowers. 'Blue Bird' has single azure-blue flowers. 'Coelestis' has large, double pale blue-violet flowers. 'Woodbridge' has large pink flowers with red centers. The Goddess series of triploids, developed at the U.S. National Arboretum, has extremely large flowers, but the plants are slightly less cold-hardy, only to Zone 6. 'Aphrodite' has rose-pink flowers with red eyes; 'Diana', pure white; 'Helene', white with deep red centers; and 'Minerva', lavender-pink with red centers.

RELATED SPECIES: *H. rosa-sinensis* (Chinese hibiscus) is a large shrub, 10 to 15 feet tall and nearly as wide, with spectacular 4- to 8-inch flowers. It can be left outdoors in Zones 10+ as a screen planting, espalier, or specimen for accent. In colder zones it can be planted in a large container, kept pruned, and moved indoors during cold weather. There are many cultivars with white, pink, red, orange, yellow, or apricot flowers.

Hibiscus syriacus *'Aphrodite'*

Hibiscus rosa-sinensis *'Fifth Dimension'*

HYDRANGEA ARBORESCENS

hy-DRAIN-ja ar-bor-ESS-ens

Smooth hydrangea

- **White flowers in 4- to 6-inch flat or globose clusters, early to late summer**
- **Bold foliage texture**
- **Low shrub**
- **Zones 3 to 9**

Hydrangea arborescens *'Annabelle'*

This low shrub, native to the eastern and central United States, has flattened clusters of mostly fertile flowers in the wild, but cultivars have been selected for all-sterile snowball-type clusters. In the North, it dies down over winter. Elsewhere, the stems can be cut back to stubs in spring to maintain the low form.

USES: Front of the shrub border, or for low massing or informal hedging.

CULTURE: Best in good garden soil but does well almost anywhere—in full sun in cool climates to considerable shade, especially in the South.

CULTIVARS: 'Annabelle' is similar but more spectacular, with clusters 8 to 12 inches across, nearly hiding the foliage.

RELATED SUBSPECIES AND SPECIES: *H. arborescens* ssp. *radiata* (silverleaf hydrangea), native to the Carolinas, is similar to the species except that its leaves are silvery white fuzz underneath. It is rarely available, but useful in naturalizing in its native range or elsewhere.

H. paniculata (panicle hydrangea), a Japanese species, is a shrub to 15 feet, traditionally seen as the selection 'Grandiflora' (peegee hydrangea), with pyramidal flower clusters, to 10 inches long, white in midsummer and turning pinkish with age. The selection 'Praecox' starts to flower about three weeks earlier than the species, with a few more large, sterile flowers. 'Tardiva' flowers later than the species, with tiered clusters of small and large flowers. Several new selections have just entered the nursery trade, including 'Burgundy Lace', with pale pink flowers that turn mauve with age, and 'Pink Diamond', with large clusters of pink buds opening white, then turning a rich pink.

HYDRANGEA MACROPHYLLA

hy-DRAIN-ja MAC-ro-FILL-a

Bigleaf hydrangea

- **Big, bold clusters of pink, blue, or mauve flowers in summer**
- **Lustrous bright green leaves**
- **Rounded shrub 3 to 5 feet tall**
- **Zones 7 to 10, mild part of Zone 6**

Flower color depends on soil acidity: blue in acidic soil (below pH 5.5) or pink at pH 6.2 and above. Some cultivars color best in only one range; others are effective in both. Flower clusters are of two types. The flattish lacecap form, with small fertile flowers surrounded by a ring of large sterile flowers, is that of the wild species. In the globose Hortensia form, all the flowers are large and sterile.

USES: Specimen for accent, or the front of a shrub border.
CULTURE: Best in fertile, well-drained soils. Water during severe drought. Plant in full sun, or half shade where summers are hot. Add lime to acidic soils for pink flowers. Maintaining pink color is tricky, because the upper limit for good growth of most cultivars is pH 6.5, leaving a narrow pH range (6.2 to 6.5) for both pink color and good growth. In the transition range (pH 5.5 to 6.2), flowers of some cultivars are a muddy mauve.
VARIETIES AND CULTIVARS: The var. *macrophylla* includes the Hortensia types: 'All Summer Beauty', is a compact repeat bloomer that looks good even in the transition zone, with a pleasing mixture of blue and pink. 'Nikko Blue' is the most popular blue form, with deep blue flowers in acidic soil.

The var. *normalis* includes the lacecap cultivars: 'Mariesii' functions well in both the blue and pink ranges. 'Mariesii Variegata' has ivory-variegated leaves.

Hydrangea macrophylla *'Blue Wave'*

Hydrangea macrophylla *Pink 'n Pretty*™

HYDRANGEA QUERCIFOLIA

hy-DRAIN-ja quare-si-FOL-ee-a

Oakleaf hydrangea

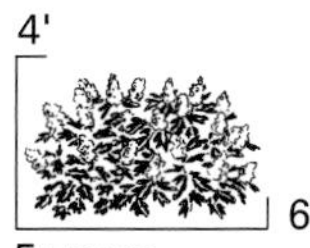

- **Pyramidal clusters of white flowers, to 10 inches long, in early summer**
- **Large oak-shaped leaves turn mahogany red in autumn**
- **New stems covered with dense mat of reddish brown hairs**
- **Zones 5 to 9**

This native of the southern Appalachian plateau is a superb, mounded foliage plant that grows 6 to 8 feet tall in full sun in Zones 7 and 8. Tops are sometimes winter-killed in Zones 5 and 6, which eliminates flowering the next year, but plants return to 3 to 4 feet in one season, and the 8-inch leaves provide strong textural interest and autumn color even in the absence of flowers. This shrub is best known for its large pyramidal clusters of creamy white flowers in early summer, turning pink by late summer, then brown in autumn.
USES: Specimen, border shrub, or massed for effect.
CULTURE: Does well in any good garden soil, even if on the wet side, in full sun for best flowering. Tolerates half shade.
CULTIVARS: 'Alice' is a full-sized selection with large flower clusters that flush pink as they age and outstanding burgundy-red autumn foliage. 'Joe McDaniel' is extremely vigorous, with large flower clusters and deep green leaves that color well. 'Pee Wee' and 'Sikes Dwarf' are dwarf selections 3 to 4 feet tall. 'Snow Queen' is a popular selection with large clusters of white flowers that turn pink as they mature and deep red-bronze autumn foliage. 'Snowflake' is a vigorous selection with unusual double individual flowers, unlike those of any other cultivar.

Hydrangea quercifolia *'Snowflake'*

Hydrangea quercifolia *'Snow Queen'*

HYPERICUM FRONDOSUM

hy-PARE-i-cum fron-DOE-sum

St. Johnswort

Hypericum frondosum

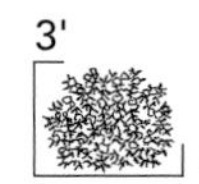

- **1- to 2-inch golden flowers, mid- to late summer**
- **3- to 4-foot mounded shrub with rich green deciduous leaves**
- **Zones 5 to 9**

This native of the eastern United States provides strong yellow flowering interest in summer.

USES: Specimen, front of a shrub border, or massing.

CULTURE: Best in well-drained garden soil in full sun or light shade.

CULTIVAR: 'Sunburst' grows less than 3 feet tall, with lots of flowers and blue-green foliage that turns orange-red in autumn in some years.

RELATED SPECIES AND CULTIVARS: *H. calycinum* (Aaronsbeard St. Johnswort) is a 1-foot mat of rich green leaves with 2- to 3-inch golden flowers. Good ground cover for Zones 6 to 9; evergreen in Zones 7 to 9.

H. 'Hidcote' has ascending stems to 3 feet and showy 2-inch flowers. Useful in Zones 5 to 9 but subject to winter dieback in Zones 5 and 6, returning to flower by middle to late summer.

H. kalmianum (Kalm St. Johnswort) is a deciduous 3-foot shrub with narrow leaves and small but profuse flowers in midsummer. It is the best St. Johnswort for the far north, including Zone 4.

IBERIS SEMPERVIRENS

eye-BEER-iss sem-per-VIE-rens

Evergreen candytuft

Iberis sempervirens *'Snowmantle'*

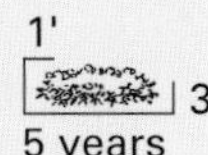

- **Pure white flowers in small clusters, late spring**
- **Mat of fine-textured evergreen foliage to 10 inches tall**
- **Narrow, leathery dark green leaves**
- **Zones 5 to 7**

This mat-forming evergreen shrub from the Mediterranean region is troublefree and delightful in flower, some cultivars flowering a second time in autumn. Shearing it back after flowering promotes new, cleaner-looking growth.

USES: Ground cover, front of the shrub border, rock garden specimen.

CULTURE: Grows well in well-drained garden soil in full sun to half shade.

CULTIVARS: 'Alexander's White', 'Purity', and 'Snowflake' are a few of the best for heavy spring flowering. 'Autumn Beauty', 'Autumn Snow', 'Christmas Snow', and 'October Glory' flower a second time, in early autumn. 'Kingwood Compact' and 'Little Gem' are lower, growing only 4 to 6 inches tall. 'Snowmantle' is unusually vigorous, growing 12 to 15 inches high.

RELATED SPECIES: *I. saxatilis* (rock candytuft) has narrower leaves and stays under 6 inches. White flowers are tinged purple with age. Zone 6.

ITEA VIRGINICA

eye-TEE-a ver-JIN-i-ka

Virginia sweetspire

Itea virginica *'Henry's Garnet'*

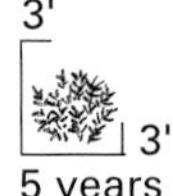

- **Creamy white flowers, early summer**
- **Irregular, 3- to 5-foot shrub**
- **2- to 4-inch leaves turn crimson in autumn**
- **Zones 6 to 9**

The fragrant flowers, in 4- to 6-inch erect spikes, are delightful but surpassed for color by the intensely red fall foliage. Otherwise nondescript, sweetspire is worth using for its fall color and tolerance of wet soil.

USES: Shrub border or low mass.

CULTURE: Best in moist soil; doesn't fare well in dry sites where it may need occasional irrigation. Avoid really dry sites. Tolerates full sun or shade but may lose seasonal color in deep shade.

CULTIVARS: 'Henry's Garnet' is a superior selection for flowering and autumn foliage. 'Sara Eve' has soft purplish-pink flowers and reddish new growth. 'Saturnalia' is noted for its multicolored autumn foliage: red, orange, pink, and yellow. 'Sprich' (Little Henry™) is a compact dwarf, growing to 2 feet tall and 3 feet wide.

RELATED SPECIES: *I. japonica* (Japanese sweetspire) is similar but taller, with softer autumn color. 'Beppu' is 2 to 3 feet tall, with wine-red autumn foliage.

JACARANDA MIMOSIFOLIA

jack-a-RAN-da mi-MOSE-i-FOL-ee-a

Jacaranda

- **Blue-violet flowers, late spring into summer**
- **Doubly compound leaves**
- **Rounded, open habit**
- **Zone 10+, mildest Zone 9**

This showy tree from Brazil, growing 25 to 50 feet tall, has an awkward growth habit, often bending to one side, with sparse branching. Its doubly compound bright green leaves produce a fine, fernlike texture, each leaf comprising more than 200 tiny leaflets. The leaves are semievergreen, gradually falling away to offer more winter light. The tree is spectacular in late spring, when its 2-inch trumpetlike flowers open in loose pyramidal clusters 8 inches high; flowering continues into summer.
USES: Shade or avenue tree, specimen for accent and contrast, or lawn tree for filtered shade in summer. Mulching minimizes turf competition.
CULTURE: Best in well-drained, light, sandy soil. Flowers heavily in full sun, but will tolerate shade. It is notoriously intolerant of salt.
CULTIVAR: 'Alba' is seldom available. Other selections have been made for form and flowering but often are not named.

Jacaranda mimosifolia

JASMINUM SPECIES

jazz-MINE-um

Jasmine

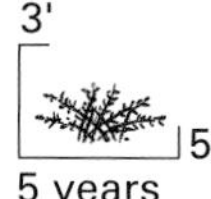

- **Fragrant flowers, spring or summer**
- **Weakly climbing or trailing habit**
- **Most with evergreen foliage**
- **Hardiness varies with species**

These scrambling shrubs and climbers have fragrant flowers, some quite showy. Most are evergreen.
USES: Shrub border, climbers for accent and fragrance.
CULTURE: Needs well-drained, slightly acidic soil (not above pH 6.5) in full sun or light shade.
SPECIES: *J. beesianum* (pink jasmine), from western China, forms a 3-foot mound, or to 6 feet high with support, with deep pink flowers. Hardy in Zones 8 and 9 and mild parts of Zone 7.

J. floridum (flowering jasmine), from China, makes a mounded shrub to 3 feet high and wider, with fragrant yellow flowers in terminal clusters. It is hardy in the same zones as *J. beesianum*.

J. nudiflorum (winter jasmine) is deciduous to semievergreen, with bright yellow flowers. A vigorous scrambler and effective bank cover, it is useful in Zones 7 to 9 and sheltered sites in Zone 6.

Jasminum nudiflorum

KALMIA LATIFOLIA

KAL-mee-a lat-i-FO-lee-a

Mountain laurel

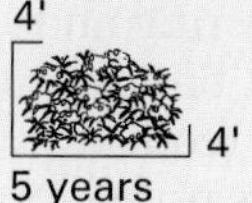

- **Showy white, pink, rose, or purple flowers, early summer**
- **Compact evergreen**
- **Needs well-drained, acidic soil**
- **Zones 5 to 8**

This remarkable evergreen shrub, native to the eastern states, grows 6 to 8 feet tall and nearly as wide under good conditions. It has distinctive bowl-shaped flowers in white, many shades of pink and rose, and in some cultivars bicolored, opening after the spring flush of azalea and rhododendron flowers.
USES: Specimen, screen, ericaceous border, or naturalized.
CULTURE: Must have acidic soil, not over pH 5.5. Best flowering in full sun in the North but needs at least light shade where summers are hot. Performs best in cool sites.
CULTIVARS: At least 50 have been introduced since 1980. 'Heart of Fire', 'Richard Jaynes', and 'Sarah' have red buds opening pink to rose. 'Ostbo Red' has red buds opening very pale pink. 'Minuet' and the dwarf 'Elf' have pink buds opening white. 'Pristine' and 'Snowdrift' have pure white flowers. 'Raspberry Glow' has maroon buds opening deep raspberry pink.

Kalmia latifolia *'Ostbo Red'*

KERRIA JAPONICA

CARE-ee-a ja-PON-i-ca

Kerria

Kerria japonica *'Pleniflora'*

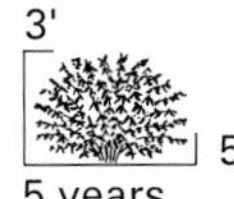

- **Golden-yellow flowers, midspring**
- **Crisp bright green leaves**
- **Stems remain green in winter**
- **Zones 5 to 9**

This shrub from China has gracefully arching pea green branches about 5 feet tall. Its leaves remain bright green after most others have darkened, and its green stems provide winter interest. The nearly 2-inch flowers, borne in abundance, make this one of the showiest flowering shrubs.

USES: Effective as a facing shrub for the front of the border, as a specimen for accent, or in massing.

CULTURE: Grows in any good garden soil, even if not perfectly drained, in full sun or considerable shade.

CULTIVARS: 'Albiflora' has creamy yellow flowers. 'Golden Guinea' has unusually large single flowers. 'Pleniflora' has large, ball-shaped double flowers that persist longer than single flowers and turn deeper yellow. 'Variegata' ('Picta') is a smaller plant with white-variegated leaves, best used in smaller-scale situations. Green-leaved shoots should be removed promptly.

KOELREUTERIA PANICULATA

kole-roo-TEER-ee-a pan-ik-yew-LAY-ta

Golden rain tree

Koelreuteria paniculata

- **Yellow flowers, summer**
- **Small to medium-sized round-headed tree**
- **Striking papery fruiting pods**
- **Zones 6 to 9, milder parts of Zone 5**

This handsome tree from China and Korea grows to 25 feet tall and as broad, with 1-foot compound leaves giving it a shaggy look. By middle to late summer, the crown is covered with bright golden yellow flowers in large clusters, which are soon followed by papery pale green fruiting pods that appear to be inflated. The pods turn tan, dry to warm brown, and hang on the tree through autumn.

USES: Shade tree or lawn specimen, or accompanying a shrub border.

CULTURE: This tree tolerates almost any well-drained soil and hot, dry summers. Full sun promotes the greatest flowering, but the tree will take light shade.

CULTIVARS: Although most trees begin to flower by midsummer, some flower as long as six weeks later. The selection 'September', found on the Indiana University campus by the late J. C. McDaniel of the University of Illinois, starts to flower in late August or early September.

KOLKWITZIA AMABILIS

kolk-WITZ-ee-a a-MAH-bil-iss

Beautybush

Kolkwitzia amabilis

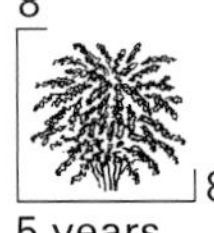

- **Profusion of pale pink flowers, late spring**
- **Large shrub (to 10 feet tall and wide) with arching branches**
- **Tan bark peels off in large strips**
- **Zones 5 to 8**

This fast-growing native of northern China is one of the showiest of all flowering shrubs. A profusion of pale pink flowers covers the graceful branches in late spring, giving a fountainlike appearance. After flowering, the medium-green foliage is attractive but, like the small, bristly fruits, is not a landscape asset. The shedding bark gives the plant a ragged appearance in winter. At full size, this shrub occupies a circle 10 to 12 feet in diameter, so it is not a logical choice for a small property.

USES: Back of the shrub border, or as a specimen for accent.

CULTURE: Needs regular renewal pruning after it has grown to size, but little other care. Tolerates almost any soil, even without the best drainage, and grows well in full sun to half shade.

CULTIVAR: 'Pink Cloud' has deep pink flowers.

LABURNUM X WATERERI

la-BURN-um WOT-er-er-eye

Goldenchain tree

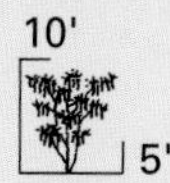
10' 5' 20 years

- Hanging chains of bright yellow flowers, late spring
- Large shrub or small tree
- Bright green leaves, green bark
- Zones 6 and 7; cool summers in Zone 8

This small tree, a hybrid of two European species, is stiffly upright at first, usually growing 15 to 20 feet tall and eventually spreading. Its 1-inch flowers, in chains 10 to 20 inches long, are the reason for its popularity.

USES: Lawn or patio tree, or included in a shrub border.

CULTURE: Best in well-drained soil, in full sun or partial shade. It is subject to trunk scald, so the trunk should be wrapped for a year or two after transplanting. Very windy sites may foster summer leaf-scorch.

CULTIVAR: 'Vossii' is full and has long flower chains.

RELATED SPECIES: The parents of this hybrid are *L. anagyroides* and *L. alpinum*. The former, from lowlands in southern Europe, is less cold-hardy, and has shorter flower chains. *L. alpinum* (Scotch laburnum), from higher elevations, is slightly more cold-hardy, with long flower chains, but it is not widely available.

Laburnum × watereri *'Vossii'*

LAGERSTROEMIA INDICA

lay-ger-STREEM-ee-a IN-di-ka

Crape myrtle

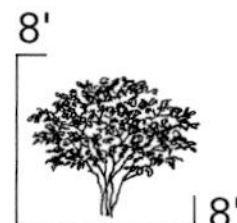
8' 8' 20 years

- Showy flowers, mid- to late summer
- Deciduous shrub or small tree
- Neat oval leaves unfold bronze, turn green, then color in autumn
- Sculpted trunk, bicolored bark
- Zones 7 to 9+

This Chinese tree is prized for its brilliant summer flowers and the architecture of its trunks and branches. Flower colors range from red, pink, and white to lavender, and sizes from dwarf or pendulous shrubs 3 feet tall to multiple-trunked trees growing to 20 feet tall. Crape myrtle is prone to mildew; when selecting, consider size and disease-resistance first, then color.

USES: Specimen, screen, or as part of a shrub border.

CULTURE: Crape myrtles need well-drained soil and full sun. They do well in heat but not in extended drought. Each spring, remove spent flower clusters and deadwood.

CULTIVARS: Many of the best mildew-resistant cultivars have come from the U.S. National Arboretum and are named after Native American tribes, but there are other fine cultivars as well, especially dwarf and pendulous selections.

Lagerstroemia indica *'Seminole'*

LAVANDULA ANGUSTIFOLIA

la-VAN-dew-la ang-gus-ti-FOL-ee-a

English lavender

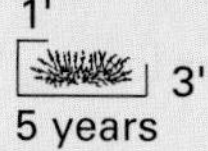
1' 3' 5 years

- Fragrant blue-lavender to purple flowers in spikes, early to late summer
- Aromatic evergreen leaves
- Zones 6 to 8, some to milder parts of Zone 5

This charming small shrub with semievergreen gray-green foliage grows from 18 inches in Zone 5 to 2 to 3 feet in Zones 7 and 8.
Its fragrant lavender-purple flowers are best in a mass planting or low hedge, to build a mass of fragrance, and its foliage is fragrant when crushed or brushed against.

USES: Excellent as an edging. You can extend its general color by planting it with grape hyacinths and dwarf asters. It is also useful in the rock garden, in the front of a border, or as a small-scale ground cover.

CULTURE: Winter hardiness can be a problem in Zone 5. You can give some protection with a loose mulch, but replacements should be planted in full sun in well-drained soil; it doesn't matter if the soil is a little dry.

CULTIVARS: 'Alba' has white flowers. 'Hidcote', 'Munstead', and 'Nana' are compact, to 18 inches tall, and cold-hardy to Zone 5.

Lavandula angustifolia

LEPTOSPERMUM SCOPARIUM

LEP-to-SPERM-um sko-PAIR-ee-um

New Zealand tea-tree

Leptospermum scoparium *'Ruby Glow'*

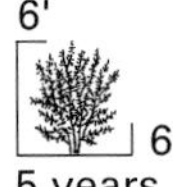

- **White, pink, or red flowers, late winter into summer**
- **Small, aromatic evergreen leaves**
- **Densely compact, upright shrub 6 to 10 feet tall**
- **Zones 9 and 10**

This native of Australia and New Zealand bears abundant flowers from late winter to midsummer.
USES: As specimen for accent, shrub border, or visual screen.
CULTURE: Drought-tolerant once established but needs water until then. Not tolerant of poor drainage or alkaline soil. Prefers full sun and only light tip pruning.
CULTIVARS: 'Blossom' is upright with double coral-pink flowers. 'Crimson Glory' is compact with double bright crimson flowers. 'Gaiety Girl' grows to 5 feet with lavender-tinted double pink flowers. 'Keatleyi' has silky red-tinted young growth and large single pink flowers. 'Nanum' is a dwarf shrub (to 2 feet) with single pink flowers and bronze leaves. 'Pink Cascade' has a weeping habit and pink flowers. 'Red Damask' has double ruby-red flowers and red-tinged new leaves. 'Ruby Glow' has dark green foliage and dark red flowers. 'Snow White' is a compact, spreading plant to 4 feet with double white flowers.

LEUCOPHYLLUM FRUTESCENS

LOO-co-FILL-um froo-TESS-senz

Texas ranger

Leucophyllum frutescens

- **Showy pink or purple flowers, midsummer or following rain**
- **Shrub 5 to 10 feet tall and nearly as wide, evergreen or nearly so**
- **Small leaves silvery-felted underneath**
- **Zones 8 to 10**

This native of Texas and Mexico is a compact, rather slow-growing shrub with excellent foliage color during the growing season, dulling by late winter.
USES: Hedge, screen, dry border.
CULTURE: Needs good soil drainage; tolerates alkaline soils, dryness, wind, and desert heat. Needs careful watering for establishment but avoid overwatering.
CULTIVARS: 'Compactum' has pink flowers and grows to 5 feet tall and wide. From Texas A&M University come 'Green Cloud', with deep green foliage and pink flowers, and 'White Cloud', with white flowers.
RELATED SPECIES: *L. candidum* (silver sage) is slightly smaller than Texas ranger, with more intensely silvered leaves. 'Silver Cloud' is compact, growing to 5 feet tall, with blue-purple foliage. 'Thunder Cloud' is similar but grows to only 3 feet tall and wide.

LEUCOTHOE FONTANESIANA

loo-KO-tho-ee fon-ta-neez-ee-AY-na

Drooping leucothoe

Leucothoe fontanesiana

- **Small waxy-white flowers in drooping spikes to 3 inches long, late spring**
- **Graceful low evergreen shrub**
- **Leathery dark green leaves turn bronze-purple in winter sun**
- **Zones 5 to 8**

This member of the heath family *(Ericaceae)* from the southern Appalachians grows to 5 feet tall and wider in time. Its 3- to 6-inch long-pointed leaves, in a double row along the arching stems, are attractive, as are its ivory, lily-of-the-valleylike flowers.
USES: Massing, especially as facing shrubs in front of rhododendrons.
CULTURE: Needs well-drained acidic soil with plenty of organic matter such as peat moss. Grows well in complete shade to nearly full sun. Summer shade is desirable in the South, and some winter shade helps to avoid leaf scorch in the North.
CULTIVARS: 'Rainbow' ('Girard's Rainbow') grows slowly to 4 feet, with attractive tricolored foliage. 'Zebonard' (Lovita™) has smaller leaves and makes a mound 2 feet high and twice as wide. 'Zeblid' (Scarletta™) grows to 3 feet tall, with scarlet new growth that turns dark green, then deep red-purple in autumn.

LONICERA FRAGRANTISSIMA

lo-NISS-er-a fray-gran-TISS-i-ma

Winter honeysuckle

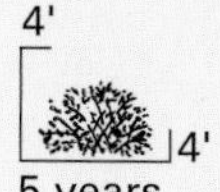

- **Fragrant white flowers, early spring**
- **Compact shrub to 6 feet**
- **Semievergreen blue-green leaves**
- **Zones 5 to 8**

Winter honeysuckle is showy because it blooms before the foliage unfolds. Its handsome, leathery leaves remain blue-green until late autumn.

USES: Good as a hedge or background or in a shrub border.

CULTURE: Any garden soil will do, even if not perfectly drained. As an informal hedge, honeysuckle needs only one pruning, after flowering in spring. For a formal hedge, it needs a repeat shearing or two, but it will be at the expense of flowering. Avoid pruning after midsummer.

RELATED SPECIES: *L. pileata* (privet honeysuckle) has 1-inch evergreen leaves on arching stems and small fragrant white flowers in spring followed by translucent violet fruits. It makes a good informal hedge 2 to 3 feet high and is useful in Zones 7 to 10. *L. nitida* (boxleaf honeysuckle) has smaller evergreen leaves and slightly larger flowers. It grows 4 to 6 feet tall in Zones 8 to 10.

Lonicera fragrantissima

LONICERA TATARICA

lo-NISS-er-a ta-TAR-i-ca

Tatarian honeysuckle

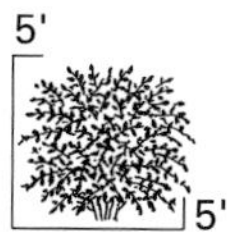

- **White, pink, or red flowers, late spring**
- **Tall shrub (to 10 feet)**
- **Red berries, late summer**
- **Zones 4 to 8, part of Zone 3**

This Asian shrub has been a mainstay in the Far North, but most cultivars are found to be susceptible to the destructive honeysuckle aphid, first noted in 1981.

USES: Screen or shrub border.

CULTURE: Grows in full sun to light shade in almost any soil, with occasional renewal pruning.

CULTIVARS: 'Arnold Red' has deep red flowers and is resistant to the honeysuckle aphid. 'Honeyrose', a hybrid between 'Arnold Red' and 'Zabelii' from the University of Minnesota, is rapidly replacing the susceptible cultivars.

RELATED SPECIES: *L. xylosteum* 'Nana' (emerald mound) makes a low mound of dark green foliage, to 3 feet high. *L × xylosteoides* 'Clavey's Dwarf', a hybrid of *L. tatarica* and *L. xylosteum*, is more compact than *L. tatarica*, to 6 feet tall but easily kept lower. Both are resistant to the aphid.

Lonicera tatarica *'Arnold Red'*

LOROPETALUM CHINENSE

lor-o-PET-a-lum chy-NEN-see

Fringe flower

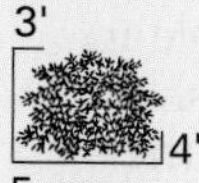

- **Creamy white, pink, or red flowers, midspring**
- **Evergreen leaves are dark green in winter**
- **Broadly rounded shrub reaching 8 feet tall and wider with arching branches**
- **Zones 8 to 10**

This handsome relative of the witch hazels (sometimes called evergreen witch hazel) bears spidery white flowers that show to good advantage against the dark foliage.

USES: Screen, shrub border, or espalier.

CULTURE: Best in moist, well-drained soil, and in partial to heavy shade.

CULTIVARS: Pink- to red-flowering plants are included in f. *rubrum*. Several clonal selections have been made. 'Blush' has burgundy-rose flowers and burgundy-flushed foliage. 'Burgundy' is similar but with bright pink flowers. 'Fire Dance' has rose-red flowers. 'Monraz' (Razzleberri™) is compact, with raspberry-red flowers and burgundy foliage, and blooms repeatedly during the year. 'Hillier' and 'Snow Dance' are compact white-flowering forms, growing to just 4 feet high and somewhat wider.

Loropetalum chinense *f.* rubrum

MAGNOLIA ACUMINATA

mag-NOL-ee-a a-KEW-min-ATE-a

Cucumbertree magnolia

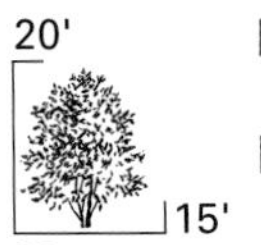

20 years

- Yellowish-green flowers in midspring
- Stately deciduous tree 60 to 90 feet tall
- 8- to 10-inch deep green leaves fall without color change
- Branches and twigs silvery gray
- Zones 5 to 8, mildest parts of Zone 4

Magnolia acuminata hybrid

This native of eastern North America is the largest and most cold-hardy of our native magnolias. It ranges from New York and Georgia to Illinois and Arkansas.

USES: A valuable but massive lawn shade tree, the species is not as showy in flower as the var. *subcordata*.

CULTURE: Thrives in any good garden soil, even if not perfectly drained, in full sun or partial shade.

VARIETIES: The var. *subcordata* (yellow cucumbertree), native to Georgia, is smaller, normally growing about 35 feet tall, although some trees have far surpassed that in old age. Its clear light yellow flowers are early enough to be visible among the immature leaves. 'Butterflies' and 'Golden Glow' are selections with deeper yellow flowers, and 'Miss Honeybee' has large pale yellow flowers.

HYBRIDS: M. × *brooklynensis* (Brooklyn hybrids), developed at the Brooklyn Botanic Garden, are hybrids between M. *acuminata* and M. *liliiflora*. The first generation of these hybrids is being used to breed additional promising cultivars.

In the search for yellow-flowered magnolias, other species, such as M. *stellata* and M. × *soulangiana*, have been hybridized with M. *acuminata*, and another group of hybrids has emerged: 'Elizabeth', a hybrid between M. *denudata* and M. *acuminata*, is a small, shrubby tree, 15 feet tall, with large ivory-yellow flowers, which it bears at an early age. It is hardy in Zones 6 to 8 and the mildest parts of Zone 5. 'Goldstar' is a densely branched, symmetrical shrub with star-shaped yellow flowers and bronzed new growth. 'Yellow Bird' is a promising hybrid between M. *acuminata* and M. × *brooklynensis*, destined to become a large tree with very showy yellow flowers.

MAGNOLIA GRANDIFLORA

mag-NO-lee-a grand-i-FLOR-a

Southern magnolia

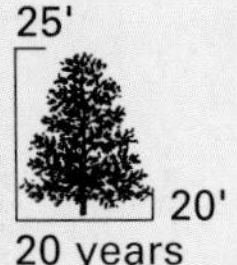

20 years

- Fragrant, 6- to 8-inch white flowers, late spring and intermittently in summer
- Large tree (60 to 70 feet tall)
- 8-inch dark evergreen leaves
- Moderate to fast growth
- Zones 7 to 10

Magnolia grandiflora

Southern magnolia is a spectacular native tree. With large, lustrous, and leathery foliage and sheer mass, it makes a bold statement wherever it grows.

USES: Large-scale shade tree, specimen or massed.

CULTURE: Should be planted in the available soil, even if not perfectly drained, and away from sweeping winds. Light to moderate shade reduces drought stress and foliage scorch, especially in Zones 7 and 8.

CULTIVARS: Many cultivars are available. Bracken's Brown Beauty® has brown-felted leaf undersides and grows to 20 feet. 'Edith Bogue' is unusally cold-hardy (to southern Zone 5), with a compact pyramidal shape and narrow leaves, tan underneath. 'Little Gem' is compact and narrowly upright, growing to 25 feet tall and half as wide. 'Poconos', found in the Pocono Mountains, may be hardy in the mildest Zone 6 sites. 'St. Mary' is compact, growing to about 20 feet tall and wide, and hardy in Zone 7. 'Samuel Sommer' is broadly pyramidal, growing to 30 feet tall and wide, with large brown-felted leaves and fragrant flowers 12 inches across, with extra tepals (petals and sepals).

RELATED SPECIES: M. *macrophylla* (bigleaf magnolia) grows 35 feet tall and 25 feet wide. Its papery leaves are 30 inches long, and its fragrant ivory flowers are 12 inches across. Useful in Zones 6 to 9 and part of Zone 5.

M. *ashei* (Ashe magnolia), from Florida, is similar to M. *macrophylla* but smaller in all its parts, only 20 feet tall. Useful in Southern Zones 6 to 9.

M. *tripetala* (umbrella magnolia), from the southeastern and south-central states, is similar to M. *macrophylla*. It has smaller leaves and flowers and is slightly more cold-hardy, through Zone 5.

MAGNOLIA LILIIFLORA

mag-NOLE-ee-a lil-ee-ih-FLOR-a

Lily magnolia

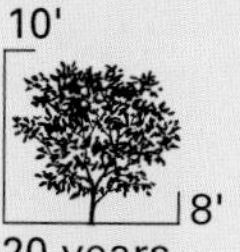

- Showy purple flowers in late spring
- Shrubby tree to 10 feet
- Later-flowering than most other Asian magnolias
- Zones 6 to 9, part of Zone 5

This Chinese magnolia is valued for its low stature and late purple flowers. It a popular breeding parent for new cultivars, including *Magnolia* × *soulangiana*.

USES: Fine tree for a small property or shrub border.

CULTURE: Like other Asiatic magnolias, it benefits from rich, well-drained soil and full sun.

CULTIVAR: 'Nigra' has deep reddish purple flowers. It opens two weeks later than saucer magnolia, so it is seldom damaged by spring frosts.

HYBRIDS: The "Little Girls", developed at the U.S. National Arboretum, are eight hybrids of M. *liliiflora* and M. *stellata*. All are small trees growing 10 to 15 feet tall and wide. Differences among them are minor, but 'Ann' is the earliest to flower, 'Betty' has the largest flowers, and 'Jane' is the latest to flower. The others are 'Judy', 'Pinkie', 'Randy', 'Ricki', and 'Susan'. All have rosy-purple flowers late enough to escape most spring frosts.

Magnolia liliiflora *'Nigra'*

MAGNOLIA X SOULANGIANA

mag-NOLE-ee-a soo-lahn-zhee-AY-na

Saucer magnolia

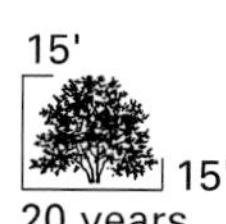

- Very showy, large pink or purple flowers, midspring
- Wide-spreading habit, to 25 feet tall and wide
- Moderately fast growing
- Zones 5 to 8, part of Zone 9

This hybrid of M. *denudata* and M. *liliflora* has fragrant 3- to 5-inch flowers, making a pink-purple mass. Its flowers are frost-nipped in some years.

USES: Showy specimen tree or accompaniment to a shrub border.

CULTURE: Planting with northern exposure slows bloom and reduces chances of freezing.

CULTIVARS: 'Alexandrina' has early, light purplish-pink flowers. 'Lennei' and 'Rustica Rubra' have late, dark red-purple flowers, whitish inside. 'Picture', introduced by Japan's Wada Nursery in the 1920s, has red-purple flowers, white inside.

RELATED SPECIES: M. *denudata* (Yulan magnolia) is a parent of saucer magnolia that grows to more than 40 feet tall. It has long been cultivated. Its ivory-white flowers are susceptible to late spring freezing in the North.

Magnolia × soulangiana

MAGNOLIA STELLATA

mag-NOLE-ee-a stel-LAY-ta

Star magnolia

- Masses of starlike pure white flowers, each with 12 to 20 or more tepals (petals and sepals), in early spring
- Compact tree 12 to 15 feet tall
- Slow-growing
- Zones 5 to 8

This shrubby tree from Japan has starlike white flowers in early spring; they are susceptible to spring frost.

USES: Specimen for accent, or part of a border.

CULTURE: Planting with a northern exposure delays flowering and avoids damage from late frosts.

CULTIVARS: 'Centennial' has 5-inch white flowers, each with 30 tepals. 'Rosea' has light pink flowers fading to white, with many tepals. 'Waterlily' flowers open white and fragrant, 5 to 6 inches across, with 20 narrow tepals.

HYBRIDS: M. × *loebneri* includes hybrids between M. *kobus* and M. *stellata*, intermediate in size with 12 tepals. 'Ballerina' functions as a larger version of M. *stellata*, to 25 feet tall with up to 30 tepals. 'Merrill' is the first cultivar from M. × *loebneri* and still one of the best, growing to 30 feet tall with white flowers. 'Leonard Messel' is open and graceful, growing 10 to 15 feet tall with clear rosy-pink flowers.

Magnolia stellata

MAGNOLIA VIRGINIANA

mag-NOL-ee-a ver-jin-ee-AY-na

Sweet bay magnolia

Magnolia virginiana

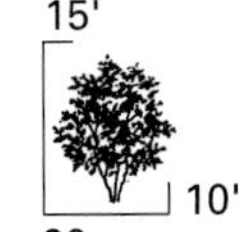

- **2- to 3-inch fragrant waxy-white flowers, late spring to early summer**
- **Dark green deciduous to evergreen leaves, sweetly aromatic when crushed**
- **Large shrub to medium tree**
- **Zone 6 to 9, part of Zone 5**

This species is native from Massachusetts to Florida and Texas along the Atlantic and Gulf coasts. Native trees are deciduous in the North, evergreen along the Gulf, and semievergreen between. They are small in the North, to 15 feet tall, but can grow to 50 feet as a tree in other parts of their range. The 3-inch flowers are not as showy as some magnolias but compensate with their fragrance.

USES: Small shade or patio tree, or in the shrub border.

CULTURE: Grows in a variety of soils, including wet sites, in full sun or partial shade but not dense shade.

VARIETIES AND CULTIVARS: The var. *australis*, growing on the southern coastal plain, is fully evergreen but not as hardy as northern material (Zones 6 to 9). 'Henry Hicks' is a superior selection, a well-shaped, medium-sized evergreen tree with large flowers.

MAHONIA AQUIFOLIUM

ma-HONE-ee-a ak-wi-FOL-ee-um

Oregon grapeholly

Mahonia aquifolium

Mahonia lomariifolia

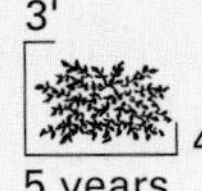

- **Bright yellow flowers, midspring**
- **Shrub to 6 feet, sometimes straggling**
- **Deep green evergreen leaves**
- **Grapelike whitish-blue fruit**
- **Zones 5 to 9**

This handsome evergreen shrub from the Pacific Northwest has lustrous compound dark green leaves with five to nine spiny leaflets reminiscent of English holly leaves. Leaves of some plants are dulled by a waxy bloom. The flower color is a bit strong, but the foliage softens it.

USES: Specimen, shrub border, or for massing; ground cover in the north.

CULTURE: Thrives in well-drained but moist situations; withstands periodic drought. Tolerates nearly full sun but is better with some shade, even nearly full shade. Full winter sun and strong winds can cause severe scorch.

CULTIVARS: 'Compacta' is low and compact, to 3 feet tall; can be kept lower with minimal pruning. Excellent as a ground cover or in a shrub border.

RELATED SPECIES: M. *bealei* (leatherleaf mahonia), from China, grows to 8 feet tall and has larger leaves, flowers, and fruits. It is upright, coarse-textured, and dramatic—a good accent plant. Its foot-long blue-green leaves have up to 15 spiny-edged leaflets, and its fragrant lemon yellow flowers are held in 6-inch upright clusters. They later hang with the weight of the fruits, pale yellowish ripening to black. This is a popular plant in Zones 7 to 9 and parts of Zone 6.

M. *lomariifolia* (Burmese or Chinese mahonia) is the most spectacular, with 20-inch green leaves composed of 25 or more leaflets and fragrant pale yellow flowers in upright spikes of up to 21 flowers each, followed by large clusters of blue-black fruits with a whitish bloom. This plant exceeds even M. *bealei* as a specimen for accent in architectural settings, but it is reliably hardy only to Zone 9.

M. *repens* (creeping mahonia), from the mountains of western North America, serves as a fair ground cover. Its dull foliage is less attractive than that of most other species, but it tolerates dry soils in Zones 5 to 7.

M. *swaseyi* (Texas mahonia) and M. *trifoliolata* (Laredo mahonia) are Texas natives and fine shrubs for semiarid climates. M. *swaseyi* grows 5 feet tall, with light blue-gray leaves, purplish in winter, and whitish-yellow fruits, flushing red. M. *trifoliolata* grows 6 feet tall, with blue-green leaves, whitened underneath, and red fruits. Both are useful in their region, Zones 7 and 8.

MALUS SPECIES AND CULTIVARS

MALE-*us*

Flowering crabapple

15' 15' 20 years

- **Showy flowers, spring**
- **Small red to yellow fruits**
- **Lustrous deep green foliage, yellow-orange in fall (some cultivars some years)**
- **Zones 4 to 8 (variable with cultivar)**

Crabapples have been improved greatly by breeding since the 1960s. Many cultivars are essentially free of apple scab disease, which can defoliate some old cultivars by late summer. Many new cultivars have very small fruits that do not pose a litter problem and in some cases remain colorful all winter. Almost every flowering crabapple puts on a fine floral display in spring. The exception is *Malus tschonoskii* (Tschonoski crab), which compensates for its weaker show of white flowers with silvery-green foliage that turns bright orange in autumn.

USES: These trees are usually grown for display by a lawn or border, but some are functional shade trees as well. A few of the smallest can serve as patio trees: 'Jewelberry'; M. *sargentii* (Sargent crabapple) and its cultivars 'Candymint', 'Pink Princess', and 'Rosea'; and the Round Table Series with Camelot-related names.

CULTURE: Crabapples do best in moderately fertile, well-drained soil and full sun or very light shade. Some need cleanup after fruiting, but most of the newer ones have very small, persistent fruit that blows away in winter or spring winds. Regular spraying is not necessary for those named here, although an occasional insect outbreak may need to be controlled.

Malus *'Strawberry Parfait'*

Malus *Sugartyme*®

Malus *'Prairifire'*

CRABAPPLE CULTIVARS

All of these have appeared on the "best" lists of specialists for superior flowering and fruiting interest and freedom from serious infections of apple scab. Many other good choices are available as well.

Cultivar	Flower	Form	Fruit	Other
'Adirondack'	White	Columnar	Orange-red	Subject to leafhoppers.
M. *baccata* var. *jackii*	White	Rounded	Dark red	Excellent foliage, coloring in fall.
'Bob White'	White	Rounded	Orange-gold	Fruits small and persistent.
'Louisa'	Pink	Spreading	Gold to orange	Weeping branches upswept at ends.
'Mary Potter'	White	Low spreading	Reddish	Wide-spreading, semiweeping.
Molten Lava™	White	Cascading	Orange-red	Heavy fruiting and yellow fall foliage.
'Ormiston Roy'	White	Broad-round	Orange-yellow	Fruits have a red blush and creamy underside.
'Prairifire'	Coral-red	Rounded	Purple-red	Spectacular bloom, fruits persist through fall.
'Red Jade'	White	Weeping	Red	Very graceful habit; fruits late summer to fall.
'Red Jewel'	White	Narrow	Cherry-red	Fruits stay colorful all winter.
M. *sargentii* 'Tina'	White	Very low	Red	Fruits colorful in late summer and early fall.
M. *sarg.* 'Candymint'	Pink	Very low	Purple-red	New foliage shiny wine-red; slow growing.
'Strawberry Parfait'	Pink	Spreading	Red-cream	New foliage red-tinted; fruits persist all winter.
Sugartyme®	White	Rounded	Bright red	Stunning floral display; fruits persist all winter.
M. *transitoria* Golden Raindrops™	White	Spreading	Yellow	Attractive cut-leaved foliage, yellow in autumn, and yellow-orange inner bark.

NANDINA DOMESTICA

nan-DYE-na do-MESS-tic-a

Heavenly bamboo

Nandina domestica

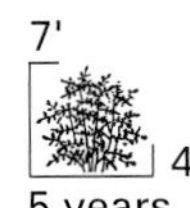

- Small white flowers in loose 12-inch clusters, late spring
- Small, pointed evergreen leaves in an open pattern
- Colorful foliage when new and in autumn
- Large clusters of red berries, autumn and winter
- Zones 7 to 9

This striking shrub has strong color and textural interest in virtually all seasons, beginning with red new foliage followed by flowers and fruits and ending with red foliage in autumn and winter.

USES: Specimen for accent, or massing or border; not full enough for screening.
CULTURE: This open shrub from China and Japan, with a bamboo-like habit, grows well in almost any garden soil, and in full sun to shade. Because of its legginess, regular pruning is needed to remove old canes and maintain good form.
CULTIVARS: 'Moyer's Red', 'Royal Princess', and 'Umpqua Chief' are colorful full-sized selections. 'Compacta' and 'Umpqua Princess' are compact-growing forms. 'Firepower', 'Harbor Dwarf', and 'Wood's Dwarf' are densely compact to 2 feet tall and wide. All but 'Umpqua Princess' have red or pink foliage in winter.

NERIUM OLEANDER

NEAR-ee-um OH-lee-an-der

Oleander

Nerium oleander

- Large clusters of red, pink, or white flowers
- Large upright shrub
- 6-inch straplike dark green leaves
- Zones 9 to 10+, sheltered in Zone 8

This shrub from the Mediterranean and Asia grows 15 feet tall and wide, with fragrant, showy single or double red, pink, white, or yellow flowers in early summer, continuing at a lesser rate until autumn. All plant parts are poisonous, even smoke from burning wood. Gloves are advised in pruning, and clippings should be disposed of carefully, not by burning.

USES: Screen, massing, border, or specimen; a good container plant.
CULTURE: Best in well-drained soil; adapted to full sun, wind, dry soil, and salt spray. Withholding moisture in late summer slows growth and promotes early hardening, especially in Zone 8.
CULTIVARS: 'Hardy Pink', 'Hardy Red', and 'Hardy White' are full-sized selections with single flowers; so is 'Calypso', with single cherry-red flowers. Intermediate-sized selections (8 to 10 feet) include 'Algiers', 'Casablanca', and 'Tangier'. 'Petite Pink' and 'Petite Salmon' are smaller, growing 6 to 7 feet tall and wide.

OXYDENDRUM ARBOREUM

ox-ee-DEN-drum ar-BORE-ee-um

Sourwood, sorrel tree

Oxydendrum arboreum

- White flowers, middle to late summer
- Pyramidal tree to 70 feet tall
- Foliage turns rich red in autumn
- Zones 6 to 8, parts of Zone 5

This deciduous member of the heath family *(Ericaceae)* is native to the Appalachians and westward to Indiana and Louisiana. Its lily-of-the-valleylike flowers hang in gracefully nodding clusters 4 to 10 inches long at a season when not many other woody plants are colorful. Its lustrous leathery leaves turn crimson to scarlet in autumn, making a fine show. It is a perfect companion to other acid-loving plants. Avoid planting in shade.

USES: Specimen, shade tree, or naturalizing.
CULTURE: This tree grows best in well-drained acidic soil (below pH 6.0 or 6.5), less acidic than is needed by many other members of the heath family. For best flowering and autumn color, it should be in full or nearly full sun.
CULTIVARS: 'Albo-marginata' has variegated leaves with white margins and some marbling, but is not widely available. 'Chameleon' has varicolored autumn foliage: red, yellow, and green.

PAEONIA SUFFRUTICOSA

pee-OWN-ee-a suf-fruit-i-CO-sa

Tree peony

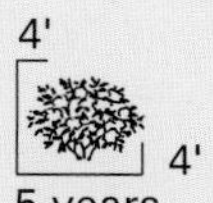

- Spectacular flowers, late spring
- Small shrub to 4 feet tall
- Dull blue-green foliage
- Zones 6 to 8, parts of Zone 5

This semiwoody perennial is grown primarily for its flowers, varying from 4 to 12 inches across, double or single, with bright yellow stamens in the center. Petal colors range from white and yellow to bronze, pink, rose, or rich red and petals are ruffled in many combinations. Flowers of some cultivars are held erect above or with the foliage, but others are partly hidden.

USES: Specimen for accent, front of the shrub border, or Oriental gardens.

CULTURE: Needs well-drained soil amended with compost or other organic matter. Does best in full sun for at least half the day, preferably in the morning, but is helped by late-day shade in areas with hot summers. Fine in full sun in cool coastal areas.

CULTIVARS: At least 150 cultivars are commercially available, mostly from peony specialists, but some cultivars are more widely available.

Paeonia suffruticosa *'Da Zong Zi'*

PARKINSONIA ACULEATA

park-in-SONE-ee-a a-kew-lee-AY-ta

Mexican palo verde

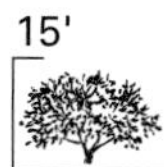

- Fragrant yellow flowers, early summer
- Fine-textured foliage
- Green bark on trunk and branches
- Zones 9 to 10+

This native of American deserts grows 20 to 30 feet tall and wide and is broadly adapted to arid areas. Its whiplike, foot-long compound leaves, with up to 50 tiny leaflets, cast very light shade. Branches are thorny. Flowers appear in clusters in late spring and early summer and intermittently thereafter.

USES: Shade or patio tree.

CULTURE: Tolerates dry, alkaline soils. Needs water at planting but seldom thereafter.

RELATED SPECIES: *P. florida* (blue palo verde, also called *Cercidium)* is equally showy in flower and similar in tolerances. *Prosopis glandulosa* (honey mesquite) is native from Kansas to the desert Southwest. Thorny and similar to *Parkinsonia,* it is a large shrub or tree 20 to 30 feet tall, casting filtered shade, bearing greenish-yellow flowers in summer.

Parkinsonia aculeata

PAULOWNIA TOMENTOSA

paul-OWN-ee-a toe-men-TOE-sa

Empress tree

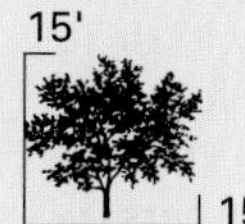

- Showy violet flowers, midspring
- Exotic-looking tree to 50 feet tall, large leaves
- Grows fast, has weak wood
- Zones 7 to 10

This native of China has escaped to the wild in the Southeast. Considered a weed, it is also a spectacular flowering tree with 10-inch leaves, much larger on young trees or following pruning. Its rapid growth, to 6 feet or more in the second or third year, makes it soft-wooded and prone to snow or ice damage. Its trumpet-shaped flowers, 2 to 3 inches long, are showy in midspring before the leaves unfold.

USES: Shade tree, especially for fast effect

CULTURE: Can grow in poor soil, but needs good drainage and full sun for best effect.

RELATED SPECIES: Three other species of *Paulownia* are uncommon in commerce: *P. fargesii,* from western China; *P. fortunei,* from China and Japan; and *P. kawakamii,* from southern China and Taiwan.

Paulownia tomentosa

PHILADELPHUS CORONARIUS

phil-a-DEL-fus co-ro-NARE-ee-us

Sweet mockorange

Philadelphus coronarius

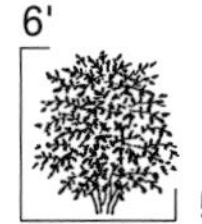

- Fragrant white flowers, late spring
- Shrub to 8 feet tall and wide
- Ordinary green foliage except for 'Aureus'
- Zones 4 to 8

This shrub from southeastern Europe, valued for the fragrance of its flowers, is especially popular in the North.

USES: Specimen, shrub border, or screen.

CULTURE: Needs well-drained soil in full sun to half shade.

CULTIVAR: 'Aureus' has bright yellow new foliage, fading gradually to green by autumn. It is good for foliage accent, growing about 6 feet tall and wide.

RELATED SPECIES AND HYBRIDS: *P. lewisii,* from the Northwest, is similar but unscented. The selection 'Waterton' is popular in the North and West. *P.* × *lemoinei* includes hybrids between *P. coronarius* and the smaller *P. microphyllus*, from the Southwest: 'Enchantment' and 'Silver Showers' grow 6 feet tall, 'Buckley's Quill' and 'Galahad' to 5 feet. The flowers of 'Buckley's Quill' are double with uniquely quilled petals. 'Miniature Snowflake' grows 3 feet tall.

PIERIS FLORIBUNDA

pee-AIR-is flor-i-BUN-da

Mountain pieris

Pieris floribunda

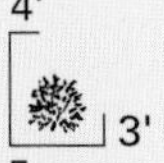

- White flowers, middle to late spring
- Spreading habit, 4 to 6 feet tall and wider
- Dark, leathery evergreen leaves
- Requires acidic soil
- Zones 5 to 7; Zone 4 with snow; Zone 8 with cool summers

This native of the southern Appalachians has flowers in semi-erect clusters, opening later than those of Japanese pieris, and is more cold-hardy.

USES: Its shape makes it useful for massing and as a specimen in the mixed border with rhododendrons.

CULTURE: Requires moist but perfectly drained soil. Slightly more shade-tolerant than Japanese pieris; neither should be planted in hot or windy sites.

CULTIVARS AND HYBRIDS: 'Millstream' grows to 2 feet tall and 3 feet wide in a decade or so, a gem in the rock garden or in front of rhododendrons. 'Brouwer's Beauty', a hybrid of *P. floribunda* and *P. japonica*, grows to 5 feet tall and broader and is useful in Zones 5 to 8 in protected sites. 'Karenoma' is a similar hybrid, about the same size as 'Brouwer's Beauty', with red winter flower buds and bronze-red new foliage.

PIERIS JAPONICA

pee-AIR-is ja-PON-i-ca

Japanese pieris

Pieris japonica *'Variegata'*

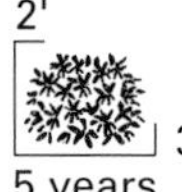

- White flowers, midspring
- Upright habit, 6 to 8 feet tall
- Lustrous evergreen foliage, colorful as it unfolds
- Requires acidic soil
- Zones 6 to 9

Its new foliage is red to chartreuse, and it has pendent 5-inch flower clusters. New flower buds are reddish in fall and winter.

USES: Specimen or in border with rhododendrons and azaleas.

CULTURE: Pieris must have well-drained, acidic soil and protection from winter sun and wind, but it needs partial sun to flower well.

CULTIVARS: 'Dorothy Wycoff' has winter buds opening pink to white and dark green foliage. 'Grayswood' has very long flower clusters. 'Mountain Fire' is compact, with bright red new foliage. 'Valley Valentine' has deep rose flowers. 'Variegata' has white-margined leaves and grows slowly.

RELATED SPECIES AND HYBRIDS: *P. formosa* var. *forrestii*, from China, is larger than Japanese pieris, useful in Zones 8 and 9 and part of Zone 7. The selection 'Wakehurst' has large leaves, bright red when immature. 'Forest Flame', a hybrid with Japaneses pieris, is similar but hardy in Zones 7 to 9.

PLUMBAGO AURICULATA

plum-BAY-go aw-rik-yew-LAY-ta

Cape plumbago

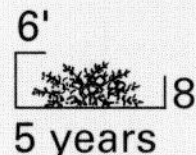

- **Masses of sky-blue flowers, early spring through fall, and all year in warmest areas**
- **Semievergreen shrub or vine**
- **Good bank or fence cover**
- **Zones 9 to 10+**

This semiclimbing plant from South Africa makes a sprawling, mounded shrub to 6 feet tall and broader in frost-free areas with some moisture; it grows shorter in dryer areas. Its blue or white flowers open almost continually in the absence of frost. Flower color varies; selecting plants that are in bloom or cultivars of known color is recommended.

USES: Erosion control on slopes; fences and walls; large-scale massing.

CULTURE: Needs well-drained soil, some water for establishment but very little thereafter. Hot sun bleaches the flower color. Plants do best in light shade or with northern exposure.

CULTIVARS: 'Alba' has white flowers. 'Imperial Blue' has deep blue flowers. 'Monott' (Royal Cape™) is vigorous, with vivid blue flowers.

Plumbago auriculata *Royal Cape*™

POTENTILLA FRUTICOSA

po-ten-TILL-a fruit-i-CO-sa

Shrubby cinquefoil

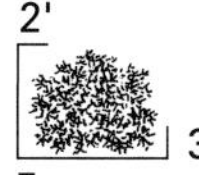

- **Yellow or white flowers most of the summer**
- **Deciduous shrub with low, compact, rounded habit**
- **Zones 3 to 7**

This shrub is a good source of color in early summer and intermittently until early autumn, even in the coldest climates.

USES: Low, informal hedge; facing shrub in a shrub border; doorway accent.

CULTURE: Does well in almost any soil that is not excessively wet or dry; prefers full sun and is fairly tolerant of seaside or deicing salts. It is at its best where summers are not too hot and dry, even though it tolerates some extremes.

CULTIVARS: 'Coronation Triumph', 'Dakota Sunrise', 'Gold Star', and 'Goldfinger' have golden yellow flowers. 'Jackmannii' has smaller numbers of large yellow flowers and excellent dark green foliage. 'Katherine Dykes' and 'Moonlight' ('Maanely's') have lighter yellow flowers. 'Primrose Beauty' has pale yellow flowers and silvery foliage. 'Abbotswood' has large, pure white flowers and outstanding blue-green foliage.

Potentilla fruticosa *'Primrose Beauty'*

PRUNUS CERASIFERA

PROO-nus sare-a-SIF-er-a

Cherry plum

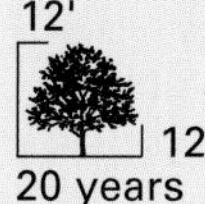

- **Light or rosy-pink flowers, early to midspring**
- **Useful small tree (15 to 20 feet tall)**
- **Red- or purple-leaved cultivars**
- **Zones 5 to 8; some cultivars to Zone 4**

These red- or purple-leaved selections of the Eurasian cherry plum are most colorful from flowering time, in early to midspring, to midsummer. Then their color fades until autumn, when some cultivars turn bright crimson. The flowers are small but offer contrast with the developing foliage.

USES: Specimen or patio tree, or an accent in a shrub border.

CULTURE: Easier to grow than other plums, and tolerant of dry soils. They should be in full sun for best leaf color.

CULTIVARS: 'Frankthrees' (Mount St. Helens®) has long-lasting leaf color, turning crimson in autumn, and is useful in Zones 4 to 8. 'Newport' is the most cold-hardy, in Zones 4 to 7. 'Thundercloud' is shapely, remaining deep purple all summer. It's hardy in Zones 6 to 8 and warmer parts of Zone 5.

Prunus cerasifera *'Thundercloud'*

PRUNUS SARGENTII

PROO-nus sar-JEN-tee-eye

Sargent cherry

Prunus sargentii

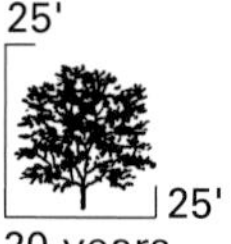

- Single rose-pink flowers, early to midspring
- Shade tree to 60 feet tall and wide
- Orange-red foliage, autumn
- Zones 5 to 8

This is the most cold-hardy of the showy Japanese cherries, and the one with the best autumn foliage color. Masses of pink flowers cover the tree before the leaves expand in midspring, then fade and drop quickly. The short bloom period of many flowering cherries is compensated for by the intensity of the spectacle.

USES: Shade tree, specimen, companion to forsythia and others in the shrub border.

CULTURE: This is one of the most trouble-free of the flowering cherries. Little pruning should be needed if enough space is allowed for this tree, which spreads to at least 40 feet. Almost any good soil, reasonably well-drained, will do. Needs good sun exposure.

CULTIVAR: 'Columnaris' is much narrower in outline than the species, usually spreading to less than 20 feet. It has all the other good traits of the species.

PRUNUS SUBHIRTELLA

PROO-nus sub-her-TELL-a

Higan cherry

Prunus subhirtella *'Pendula'*

- White to bright pink flowers, early to midspring
- Open, airy tree to 25 feet, weeping form to 20 feet
- Zones 6 to 9, milder parts of Zone 5

This graceful Japanese tree flowers before the foliage unfolds.

USES: Patio or lawn specimen.

CULTURE: Needs well-drained soil; prefers full sun or slight shade.

CULTIVARS: 'Autumnalis' grows 15 to 20 feet tall with white flowers, some opening in autumn. 'Pendula' is weeping, with single pink flowers. Other weeping cultivars have double pink or white flowers.

RELATED SPECIES AND HYBRIDS: *P.* × 'Hally Jolivette', a hybrid of *P. subhirtella* and *P.* × *yedoensis*, is a graceful shrub to 10 feet tall, with semidouble white and pink flowers opening over two to three weeks. Zones 5 to 9.

P. campanulata (Taiwan cherry) has bell-shaped white to bright pink flowers in nodding clusters. Zones 8 to 10. 'Okame', a hybrid of *P. campanulata*, is an upright small tree with long-lasting rose-pink flowers in early spring. Zones 6 to 9+.

PRUNUS TOMENTOSA

PROO-nus toe-men-TOE-sa

Nanking cherry

Prunus tomentosa

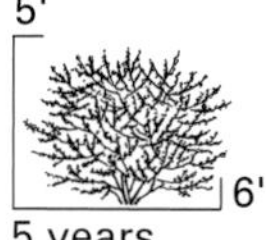

- White flowers, early spring
- Large shrub (to 10 feet tall and wider)
- Edible red fruits, "pie" cherries
- Zones 3 to 6

This bush cherry furnishes small cooking cherries in Zones 3 and 4, where it's too cold for red cherry trees. Its floral display is also much appreciated in these zones.

USES: Screen, hedge, specimen, or in a shrub border.

CULTURE: Prefers well-drained, even somewhat dry soils in full sun.

CULTIVARS: 'Geneva' has vigor and large fruits, ½ inch in diameter.

RELATED SPECIES: *P. glandulosa* (dwarf flowering almond), from China and Japan, grows 3 to 5 feet tall and broad, with showy white or pink flowers in midspring. 'Sinensis' ('Rosea Plena'), with long-lasting double pink flowers, is the showiest form of this species, often mislabeled 'Rosea'.

P. triloba (flowering almond), from China, is a larger shrub, 10 to 12 feet, usually with double pink flowers, although single-flowered plants exist. 'Multiplex' has double flowers.

PRUNUS HYBRIDS

PROO-nus

Oriental flowering cherries

- White to pink flowers, early to midspring
- Very showy hybrids
- Zones 6 to 9

These hybrids, along with the Yoshino cherries (below) and cultivars already mentioned, make up the Japanese flowering cherries that bring thousands of tourists to Washington, D.C., in April.

USES: Specimen or avenue trees, with a shrub border, and in Japanese gardens.

CULTURE: Need well-drained soil and direct sun but protection from strong winds.

HYBRID GROUPS: Cultivars in the Sato-zakura group (formerly called *P. serrulata* hybrids) flower in midspring. 'Amanogawa' is narrowly upright when young and broadens with age, with masses of fragrant semidouble flowers, translucent pale pink to white.

'Sekiyama' (Kwanzan cherry) is the most popular of these cultivars, with a vase shape and huge clusters of double bright pink flowers that remain colorful for about two weeks.

'Royal Burgundy' is similar to 'Sekiyama' but with deeper pink flowers and red-purple foliage, turning orange-red in autumn.

'Shiro-fugen' grows rapidly with a spreading habit and rosy-pink buds that open into unscented double white flowers. Its new foliage is red-orange.

'Shirotae' ('Mount Fuji') has a wide-spreading, flat-topped growth habit and large, fragrant white flowers varying from semidouble to double.

The second group of hybrids—*Prunus × yedoensis* (Yoshino or Potomac cherry)—includes the cherries that are planted around the Tidal Basin in Washington. They are hybrids of *P. subhirtella* and *P. speciosa* (Oshima cherry) and are among the showiest of flowering trees. 'Akebono' ('Daybreak') is spreading in habit and magnificent in bloom, with single, translucent soft-pink flowers. 'Shidare Yoshino' ('Pendula') is strongly pendulous in habit, with white flowers. It grows to 40 feet in time, larger than the weeping forms of *P. subhirtella*.

FLOWERING CHERRY CULTIVARS

Name	Height (feet)	Tree Form	Flowers
Taiwan cherry (*P campanulata*)	20-25	Loosely upright	White or pink, single, bell-shaped
Okame cherry (*P.* 'Okame')	20-25	Narrowly upright	Bright pink, single
Sargent cherry (*P. sargentii*)	50-60	Upright, spreading	Rose-pink, single
'Columnaris'	50-60	Narrowly upright	Rose-pink, single
Higan cherry (*P. subhirtella*)	20-25	Spreading	Pale or deep pink
'Autumnalis'	10-15	Shrubby, spreading	Pink, single
'Pendula'	15-20	Weeping	Deep pink. single
Sato-zakura hybrids			
'Amanogawa'	20-25	Narrowly upright	Fragrant, pink to white, semidouble
'Sekiyama' ('Kwanzan')	20-25	Vase-shaped	Bright pink, double
'Royal Burgundy'	20-25	Vase-shaped	Deep pink, double
'Shiro-fugen'	20-25	Upright, spreading	Pink to white, double
'Shirotae'	15-20	Spreading	Fragrant white, semidouble
Yoshino (*P. × yedoensis*)	20-30	Upright, spreading	Fragrant, light pink
Akebono ('Daybreak')	20-30	Spreading	Pale translucent pink
'Pendula'	20	Weeping	Large pink flowers

Prunus × yedoensis *'Pendula'*

Prunus *'Sekiyama' ('Kwanzan')*

Prunus *'Shirotae'*

PUNICA GRANATUM

PEW-ni-ka gran-NAY-tum

Pomegranate

Punica granatum *'Nana'*

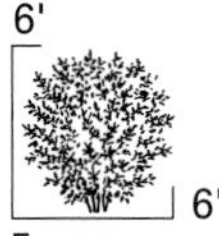

- **Colorful single or double flowers, late spring to early summer**
- **Deciduous, leathery bright green leaves, turning yellow in autumn**
- **Colorful, edible fruits**
- **Zones 8 to 10**

This compact, twiggy shrub from the Mediterranean to central Asia, growing 15 feet tall and wide over time, is interesting in most seasons for its red, yellow, or white flowers, coppery new foliage, colorful autumn foliage, or yellow fruits overlaid with red.

USES: Specimen for accent and color, hedge, or border.
CULTURE: Needs well-drained soil and full sun.
CULTIVARS: 'Alba Plena' ('Multiplex') has double white flowers, no fruits. 'California Sunset' ('Mme. Legrelle') grows 10 feet tall and wide, with semidouble coral pink and creamy white flowers. 'Chico' is low-growing, to 6 feet tall and wide, with double red-orange flowers through the summer but no fruits. 'Nana' is dwarf, growing to 4 feet tall and wide and eventually larger, with small, single orange-red flowers and smaller leaves and fruits. 'Wonderful' is a full-sized plant selected for fruit production.

PYRACANTHA SPECIES AND CULTIVARS

py-ra-CAN-tha

Firethorn

- **White flowers, early summer**
- **Prostrate to upright**
- **Semievergreen to evergreen**
- **Red to yellow berries, early autumn well into winter**
- **Zones 6 to 10, parts of Zone 5, depending on cultivar**

This shrub from southeastern Europe and Asia is irregularly open, with small flowers in large clusters, attractive against the dark green foliage. Its greatest attraction is its colorful fruit.

USES: Specimen, free-form or trained as espalier, or barrier, because of its thorns.
CULTURE: Best in well-drained soil, even if dry. Grows well and fruits in full sun to half shade. May need pruning to maintain desired habit. Susceptible to fire blight and scab, but resistant cultivars are available.
CULTIVARS: For northern climates (Zone 5): *P. coccinea* 'Kasan', 'Lalandei' and 'Lalandei Thornless' are relatively cold-hardy, growing to 5 feet or more, with orange fruits, but they are susceptible to scab. *P. angustifolia* 'Gnozam' ('Gnome') and 'Monon' (Yukon Belle™), are slightly hardier than *P. coccinea* cultivars.

For mild climates, several cultivars are highly resistant to scab and fire blight: 'Apache' is compact, 5 feet tall and wider, with bright red berries and nearly evergreen foliage, useful in Zones 7 to 10. 'Fiery Cascade' grows to 8 feet, with orange berries turning bright red in autumn. It is useful in Zones 6 to 9. 'Mohave' grows to 10 feet in time, with red-orange berries, useful in Zones 7 to 9. 'Navajo' is compact, 6 feet tall and 8 feet wide, with orange berries turning orange-red in autumn. *P.c.* 'Rutgers' is 4 feet tall and 6 feet wide, with orange berries, useful in Zones 6 to 9. *P.* 'Teton' grows to 12 feet tall and 8 feet wide, narrower while young, with bright orange berries, useful in Zones 7 to 9 and parts of Zone 6.

Pyracantha *flowers*

Pyracantha × watereri *flowers*

Pyracantha coccinea *'Lalandei'*

PYRUS CALLERYANA

PY-rus cal-er-ee-AY-na

Callery pear

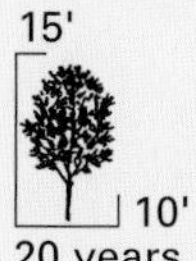
15'
10'
20 years

- White flowers, midspring
- Lustrous, leathery leaves turn mahogany-red in autumn
- Moderate to fast growth
- Zones 5 to 8

This tree from China has broad seasonal interest and fruits so small that they don't add much litter. Some cultivars produce little fruit.
USES: Shade, patio, or street tree, for shade and color.
CULTURE: Grows well in almost any well-drained soil, even if somewhat dry. Best in full sun. Corrective pruning may be needed to prevent narrow crotches in some cultivars.
CULTIVARS: 'Aristocrat' is an older selection, and the largest of this group, growing at least 50 feet tall and 35 feet wide. It bears many ½-inch fruits; its red autumn color is somewhat spotty.

'Autumn Blaze' has wide crotch angles, and its foliage colors two to three weeks earlier than that of other cultivars, suggesting earlier cold acclimation and greater hardiness, to Zone 5.

'Bradford', the first selection made from callery pear, has narrow crotches that may lead to breakage after 25 years or so, but its formal oval shape, flowering, and superb autumn foliage keep it popular even though it may be less permanent. It is not hardy in the coldest parts of Zone 5.

'Capital' is narrower, growing 30 to 35 feet tall but only about 12 feet wide, with a strong central trunk that provides structural strength.

'Chanticleer' ('Cleveland Select') is similar to 'Capital' in shape but a little larger, with excellent flowering and foliage interest.

'Redspire', a seedling of 'Bradford', grows at least 35 feet tall and 25 feet wide. It is slightly more cold-hardy than 'Bradford'.
RELATED SPECIES: *Pyrus fauriei* (Korean callery pear), once considered a variety of callery pear, is a small, round-headed tree that grows to 20 feet tall and at least as wide. Its white flowers are as showy as those of callery pear, and autumn foliage color is good in some trees. It is fully hardy in Zone 5.

Pyrus calleryana *'Bradford'*

Pyrus calleryana *'Aristocrat'*

RHAPHIOLEPIS INDICA

ray-fee-AWL-e-pis IN-di-ca

Indian hawthorn

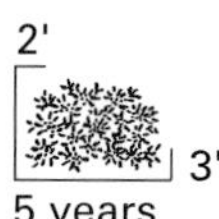
2'
3'
5 years

- White to rose flowers, late winter to early summer
- Small, rounded shrub
- Neat, dark evergreen leaves
- Zones 8 to 10

This small shrub from southern China is valued for its early and continuing flowers in all shades from white to red. Its blue-black fruits are not showy.
USES: Front of the shrub border, massing as a ground cover, or as a small informal hedge.
CULTURE: Best in well-drained soil, even if dry. Tolerates up to half shade, but growth is more compact and flowers better in full sun. It tolerates wind; good air circulation helps control leaf diseases. Does not do well in nematode-infested soil.
CULTIVARS: Several cultivars of *R. indica* and *R. × delacourii* (below) are available.
RELATED SPECIES AND HYBRIDS: *R. umbellata* (Yedda hawthorn), from Japan and Korea, is similar to Indian hawthorn except larger, to 4 feet tall, with white flowers. *R. × delacourii,* a hybrid of Indian hawthorn and *R. umbellata,* hardly differs from Indian hawthorn.

Raphiolepis indica *Majestic Beauty*™

RHODODENDRON SPECIES

roe-doe-DEN-dron

Rhododendrons and azaleas

- Extremely showy flowers, late spring and early summer
- Deciduous or evergreen
- Need well-drained acidic soil
- Zones 3 to 9, varies with species

These shrubs are favorites of gardeners who are favored with the appropriate soil and climate.
USES: The widely varied members of this species serve as ground covers, or for massing or screening, or for accent in a shrub border.
CULTURE: Most grow best in acidic (pH 4.0 to 5.5), well-drained soil rich in organic matter; some grow well in soil up to pH 6.5. Most are best in partial shade; deciduous varieties generally tolerate more sun. A few azaleas are adapted to boggy habitats, but not to heavy or poorly drained soils.

DECIDUOUS AZALEAS

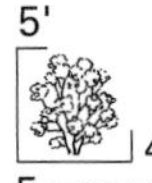
5' 4' 5 years

***R. calendulaceum* (flame azalea),** from the southern Appalachians, has yellow to orange flowers in late spring and grows to 10 feet tall. It is a parent of the popular Knapp Hill hybrids, useful in Zones 5 to 8. Related species include *R. austrinum* (Florida azalea); *R. cumberlandense* (Cumberland azalea), growing 6 feet tall in Zones 6 to 8; and *R. prunifolium*, from Alabama and Georgia, growing 12 to 15 feet in Zones 7 to 9, with red flowers.

R. calendulaceum

R. prunifolium

***R. canescens* (Piedmont azalea),** native from the Carolinas to Texas, in Zones 7 to 9, grows 10 feet tall with fragrant white-pink flowers in midspring. Its northern counterpart, *R. prinophyllum* (rose-shell azalea), growing from New Hampshire to Missouri, in Zones 4 to 6 and part of Zone 3, is a parent of the Northern Lights hybrids, which have extended the useful range of azaleas to Zones 3 and 4.

R. canescens

R. *'Apricot Sunrise' (Northern Lights hybrid)*

***R. occidentale* (western azalea),** the only native azalea west of the Rocky Mountains, is found in the mountains of California and Oregon. Its white to pinkish flowers have yellow and red markings. It is used most in its native region, Zones 7 to 9.

R. occidentale

***R. vaseyi* (pink-shell azalea),** from mountain bogs in North Carolina, grows 6 feet tall, with light rosy-pink flowers (white in 'White Find'). It is hardy in Zones 5 to 8, tolerates wet soil, and has distinctive foliage. The closely related rhodora *(R. canadens)*, a 3-foot native of boggy sites from Labrador to northern Pennsylvania (Zones 3 to 6), is purplish pink.
***R. viscosum* (swamp azalea)** grows to 8 feet tall in swamps from Maine to Alabama (Zones 4 to 9). Its pinkish white flowers in early summer are less showy than some but unexcelled for fragrance. Its mountain counterpart, *R. arborescens* (sweet azalea), grows wild from Pennsylvania to Alabama, with glossy foliage that turns red in autumn. It is less tolerant of wet soil and has deeper rose-pink flowers ('Rubescens') opening in midsummer. It is an important breeding parent for hardiness and fragrance.
***R. schlippenbachii* (royal azalea),** from Japan, grows 6 to 8 feet tall. Its 3-inch translucent pale pink flowers make a wonderful show in midspring, and its rounded leaves provide the best foliage texture of any azalea; they turn orange-red in autumn. Without flowers it would still be a striking two-season plant.

R. schlippenbachii

EVERGREEN AZALEAS

2' 4' 5 years

***R. indicum* (Indian or macrantha azalea),** from southern Japan, grows 3 to 5 feet tall, with 3-inch red flowers in late spring or early summer. It is a parent of the Southern Indian hybrids, the Glenn Dale hybrids, and the Satsuki azaleas.

Southern Indian hybrids, growing to 10 feet tall in Zone 9+ and part of Zone 8, have large flowers. Among the most popular are 'Formosa', with deep purplish-red flowers, and 'George L. Taber', with large white flowers flushed purplish pink.

Glenn Dale hybrids are useful in Zones 7 and 8, a few in Zone 6. Of some 400 cultivars introduced by the U.S. Plant Introduction Station in the 1950s, few are still available. Most grow 3 to 5 feet tall and wide. 'Fashion' has orange-red flowers in middle to late spring and arches to 6 feet tall. 'Martha Hitchcock' has 3-inch white flowers with red-purple petal margins and grows to 3 feet tall.

Satsuki azaleas, imported from Japan by the U.S. Plant Introduction Station in the 1930s, are low-growing (2 to 3 feet), with large striped or flecked flowers. They are useful in Zones 8 and 9 and parts of Zone 7. The most popular in commerce are 'Gumpo' ('Gumpo White'), with 3-inch white flowers flecked purplish pink; 'Gumpo Pink', with light pink flowers; and 'Gumpo Red', deeper rose-pink.

***R. kiusianum* (Kyushu azalea),** from Japan, grows 3 feet tall, with showy pink, purple, red, or white flowers opening with the expanding foliage in midspring. It is best known as a parent of the Obtusum and Kurume hybrids. Zones 7 to 8.

Obtusum hybrids have small, semievergreen leaves and are useful in Zones 6 to 8. 'Amoenum' has double deep magenta flowers; 'Amoenum Coccineum' has deeper red flowers.

Kurume hybrids, popular hybrids of *R. kaempferi*, *R. kiusianum*, and *R.* × *obtusum*, grow 3 to 5 feet tall and wider, making solid masses of color. Most are hardy in Zones 7 and 8 and milder parts of Zone 6. 'Coral Bells' has 1-inch bright coral-pink flowers and a spreading habit. 'Hino-crimson' has brilliant ruby-red flowers, compact growth, and superb foliage, mahogany-tinted in autumn. It is a fine plant for accent.

***R. kaempferi* (torch azalea),** a close relative of *R. kiusianum*, is taller and looser, deciduous, and cold-hardy in Zones 6 to 8. Its flowers are deep salmon-rose.

R. *'Coral bells'*

R. *'Hino-crimson'*

R. kiusianum *'Komo Kulsham'*

R. *'George L.Taber'*

R. *'Treasure' (Glenn Dale hybrid)*

RHODODENDRONS

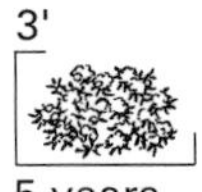

***R. carolinianum* (Carolina rhododendron),** a 5-foot native of the North Carolina mountains, has 3-inch

R. carolinianum

leaves and pink flowers in middle to late spring. A parent of the P.J.M. hybrids, it is useful in Zones 5 to 7 and parts of Zone 4.
***R. catawbiense* (Catawba rhododendron),** from the southern Appalachians, grows 6 to 10 feet tall, with lilac-purple

R. catawbiense *'Boursalt'*

flowers, white in the natural variety *album*, and is useful in Zones 4 to 7. It is also a parent of the "ironclad" Catawba hybrids, useful in Zones 6 to 8 and parts of Zone 5.
***R. fastigiatum*,** from western China, is a low plant with blue flowers, useful in Zones 6 to 8. Its hybrids, 'Purple Gem' and 'Ramapo', grow 2 to 3 feet tall,

R. *'Purple Gem'*

with small blue-green leaves and blue-purple flowers in midspring.
***R. fortunei* (fortune rhododendron),** a fragrant native of eastern China, is a parent of Dexter hybrids such as

R. *'Wheatley' (Dexter hybrid)*

'Scintillation', useful in Zones 7 to 9, where summers are moderate.
***R. maximum* (rosebay rhododendron),** a big-leaved native from Maine to Alabama,

R. maximum

grows 15 to 20 feet tall and is useful in Zones 4 to 7, blooming with the new leaves in early summer.

R. mucronulatum *'Cornell Pink'*

***R. mucronulatum* (Korean rhododendron),** one of few deciduous rhododendrons, has showy mauve flowers before the

R. *'Bruce Brechtbill'*

leaves unfold. 'Cornell Pink' has clear rosy-pink flowers.
***R. yakushimanum*,** from the mountains of southern Japan, grows 4 feet tall, with dark leaves, heavily buff-felted beneath, and pink or white flowers in midspring. Useful in Zones 6 to 8. Several fine hybrids are available.

R. yakushimanum *'Pink Parasol'*

RIBES SANGUINEUM

RYE-bees sang-GWIN-ee-um

Red-flowering currant

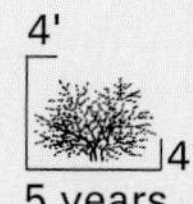

- Showy red, pink, or white flowers, middle to late spring
- Twiggy, compact habit
- Zones 6 to 10

This native of the Pacific Northwest is used mostly on the West Coast. Its flowers are usually pink to red but occasionally white.

USES: Specimen for accent, in the shrub border, or as a hedge to 6 feet tall.

CULTURE: Needs well-drained, reasonably fertile soil in full sun or moderate shade in areas with moderate summers for best flowering. Not recommended where white pines grow; it is an alternate host of white pine blister rust disease.

CULTIVARS: 'Hannaman's White', 'Spring Snow', and 'White Icicle' have white flowers effective against a dark background. 'Apple Blossom', 'Claremont', 'Emerson', and 'Pokey's Pink' have pink flowers. 'Elk River Red' and 'King Edward VII' have rosy-red flowers.

RELATED SPECIES: *R. alpinum* (alpine currant) grows to 8 feet tall and wide, with fine-textured, lobed foliage. This plant is used more for its tolerance of hot, dry sites than its beauty. Its flowers are nearly insignificant, but its foliage remains crisp and bright green during drought. It is immune to white pine blister rust. 'Green Mound' grows compactly about 4 feet tall and wide and has excellent foliage color. The dwarf form 'Pumilum', growing only about 3 feet tall, is valuable for small hedges and edgings. *R. aureum* and *R. odoratum* have fragrant yellow flowers in midspring but do not have very good form or foliage. They can be worked into a shrub border for their fragrance, away from white pines.

Ribes sanguineum

Ribes odoratum

ROBINIA PSEUDOACACIA

ro-BIN-ee-a sue-dough-a-KAY-sha

Black locust

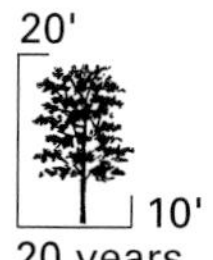

- Fragrant white flowers, very late spring
- Heavily furrowed bark
- Fast-growing, with dark green foliage
- Zones 4 to 8

This native of the east-central United States is naturalized over most of the country, southern Canada, and Europe. It drops considerable litter and small thorns, but like many other legumes, it uses atmospheric nitrogen.

USES: Shade tree; stabilizing road-cuts and other banks; in poor, dry soils.

CULTURE: Tolerates dry or alkaline soils and high winds. Trunk borers are a problem. Black locust trees may live with them for some time but are often disfigured and eventually succumb.

CULTIVARS: 'Frisia' is a smaller tree with yellow leaves that hold their color throughout the summer. It is often used for color accent and as a substitute for 'Sunburst' honeylocust. 'Umbraculifera' is a small tree with a globose head when young, later umbrella-like, seldom exceeding 15 feet in height. It is a favorite formal city tree in Europe and is used in North America on small-scale urban sites.

HYBRIDS: *R.* × *ambigua*, a hybrid with clammy locust *(Robinia viscosa)*, includes 'Idahoensis' and 'Purple Robe'. Both trees grow to 30 feet tall, with showy hanging chains of rose-purple flowers. *R. hispida* (rose acacia) is a suckering shrub forming a thicket 5 to 6 feet tall. It has rose to lavender-pink flowers in 3-inch clusters in late spring. *R.* × *margaretta* 'Casque Rouge', a hybrid of rose acacia with black locust, grows in a straggly way to 15 feet and is useful as a patio tree with showy rosy-purple flowers; but it suckers almost as much as rose acacia.

Robinia pseudoacacia

Robinia × ambigua *'Purple Robe'*

ROSA SPECIES AND HYBRIDS

RO-za

Roses

- Colorful flowers, some fragrant, spring and summer
- Prickly stems
- Vary in habit and flowering
- Wide range of hardiness

USES: Ground covers, edging, informal hedges, climbers, specimens.
CULTURE: Roses need well-drained, slightly acidic soil, amended with organic matter. Best in full sun, or light shade in the hottest climates. They need extra water in most climates, careful fertilization, and careful pruning.
CULTIVARS: There are hundreds. The type of rose first, then the cultivar should be considered in selection.

'Chicago Peace' (hybrid tea)

5' 3' 5 years

Hybrid tea roses are bred for show, one flower per stem, aiming at size and perfect flower form. They are very popular but less useful as landscape roses than many others.

3' 4' 5 years

Floribunda roses are bred for color, each stem bearing a cluster of flowers, smaller than most hybrid teas. 'Betty Prior' (medium pink) has unmistakable landscape value.

'Sunflare' (floribunda)

5' 3' 5 years

Grandiflora roses are intermediate between hybrid teas and floribundas, with many large flowers of hybrid tea form. They include 'Carrousel' (dark red), Mount Shasta' (white), and 'Queen Elizabeth' (light pink).

'Queen Elizabeth' (grandiflora)

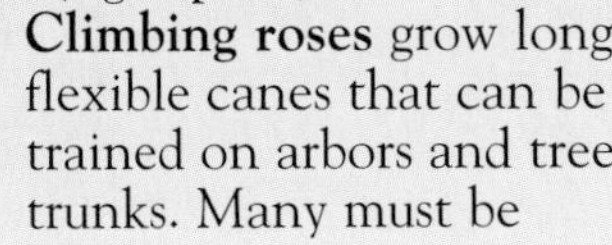

12' 3' 5 years

Climbing roses grow long, flexible canes that can be trained on arbors and tree trunks. Many must be protected over winter in Zones 3 to 5, untying canes and carefully lowering them to the ground, then covering them with loose material until early spring. A few of the best are 'Alchymist' (fragrant soft yellow), 'Blaze' (brilliant red), 'Don Juan' (fragrant deep crimson), and 'New Dawn' (fragrant pale pink).

'Don Juan' (climber)

Explorer series hybrids commemorate Canadian explorers and include several climbers hardy to Zone 4 and 5 without winter protection: 'John Cabot' (red), 'Henry Kelsey' (red), 'John Davis' (rose-pink), and 'William Baffin' (pink).

'William Baffin' (Explorer hybrid)

6' 6' 5 years

Modern shrub roses, such as the *R. rugosa* hybrids, offer hardiness and variation in size and flower color. Newer ones in the Explorer series are just as hardy and

'Country Dancer' (modern shrub)

more colorful: 'Champlain' (dark red), 'David Thompson' (fragrant pink), 'Henry Hudson' (white with yellow centers), 'Martin Frobisher' (soft pink), and others. The modern English (Austin) roses, such as

'Graham Thomas' (modern shrub)

'Abraham Darby' (very double pink), 'Fair Bianca' (very double white), and 'Graham Thomas' (very double yellow); the Romantica™ roses, from France; and the Heritage™ roses, from Denmark, are less hardy but need little winter protection in Zones 6 and warmer.

4' 6' 5 years

Old garden roses from the 19th century and earlier are still grown for their historic interest as well as fragrance and other qualities that have been de-emphasized in breeding hybrid tea roses. Their parentage includes a number of native European species. Many of them are still commercially available.

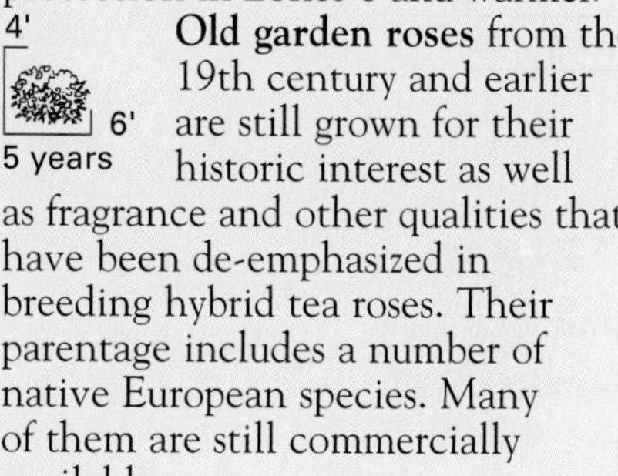

'Mme Isaac Pereire' (old garden rose; bourbon)

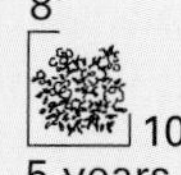
8' 10' 5 years

Species roses are wild roses either used in the wild form or in selected forms that may include a few hybrids.

R. carolina and *R. virginiana*, native to eastern North America, are useful as large-scale ground covers, 3 and 5 feet tall respectively, with single purplish-pink flowers and red fruits.

R. glauca (redleaf rose), from central Europe, has blue-green foliage, turning red-purple in sun,

R. glauca

and small pink flowers. It is cold-hardy to Zone 3 and commonly planted in shrub borders.

R. laevigata (Cherokee rose), native to China and naturalized in the South (Zones 8 and 9), is high-climbing and needs support. It has fragrant single 3-inch white flowers

R. laevigata

and semievergreen foliage and is useful for large-scale massing or barriers.

R. rugosa (rugosa rose), from eastern Asia, is naturalized in places on the North Atlantic coast; it is compact, with 3-inch purplish-pink

R. rugosa *'Alba'*

or white flowers and edible 1-inch orange-red fruits. Its wrinkled (rugose) foliage turns golden in autumn in some years.

R. setigera (prairie rose), native from Ontario and Nebraska to Florida and Texas, is a large shrub best reserved for informal use in large spaces. Its 2-inch flowers open rose, soon fading to pale pink; its foliage turns reddish-orange in autumn.

R. wichuraiana (memorial rose), a long-trailing rose from eastern Asia, has lustrous, rich green, neatly textured semievergreen foliage. Its fragrant 2-inch white flowers

R. wichuraiana

in midsummer are followed by small red fruits. It is useful for large-scale ground cover plantings or as a climber in Zones 6 to 9.

R. xanthina f. *hugonis* (Father Hugo rose) is a graceful but very prickly 6-foot shrub from central China with 2-inch butter yellow flowers in late spring and blue-green foliage. Its form is rather open because of very small leaflets. It is useful in Zones 5 to 8.

ROSMARINUS OFFICINALIS

rose-ma-RYE-nus off-fiss-in-AIL-us

Rosemary

Rosmarinus officinalis

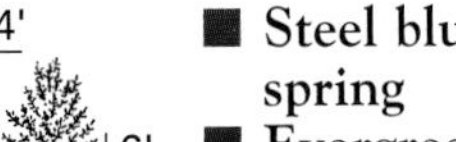

- **Steel blue flowers, late spring**
- **Evergreen shrub to 6 feet**
- **Fragrant needlelike rich green leaves**
- **Zones 8 to 10, some to Zone 7**

This compact but irregularly shaped shrub from the Mediterranean region offers unusual landscape interest and the possibility of culinary use.
USES: Edging, small hedge, specimen in shrub border or herb garden.
CULTURE: Thrives in poor and dry soils but must have good drainage. Overwatering stimulates unruly growth; needs irrigation only for establishment, and later only in a desert climate or severe drought. Tolerant of alkalinity and salt.
CULTIVARS: 'Albus' has white flowers. 'Arp' is more cold-hardy than others (Zone 7), growing to only 2 feet tall, with lighter green foliage. 'Collingwood Ingram', 'Huntington Carpet', 'Lockwood de Forest', and 'Prostratus' are low-growing selections with blue flowers. 'Huntington Carpet' spreads to 8 feet; 'Tuscan Blue' has strong vertical stems to 6 feet tall and makes a good narrow-base hedge.

SALVIA GREGGII

SAL-vee-a GREG-ee-eye

Autumn sage

Salvia greggii

- **Red flowers in loose spikes**
- **Evergreen shrub to 3 feet, with small green leaves**
- **Zones 9 and 10, and milder parts of Zone 8**

This spreading shrub or subshrub from Texas and Mexico can be grown as an herbaceous perennial in Zones 7 and 8, adding color in midsummer and fall.
USES: Mass planting or in a shrub border.
CULTURE: Tolerates dryness but does best in ordinary well-drained soil in full sun or light shade. Needs occasional renewal pruning in spring.
CULTIVARS: 'Alba' has white flowers. 'Furman's Red' has unusually bright red flowers. 'Rosea' has rose-pink to pale red flowers.
RELATED SPECIES: *S. clevelandii* (Cleveland sage), from southwestern California, has a rounded shape to 3 feet tall, fragrant gray-green foliage, and blue flowers from late spring to late summer.

S. leucantha (Mexican bush sage), a native of Mexico, grows to 3 feet, with silvery-green leaves and long, velvety bright purple flower spikes from which small white flowers emerge continuously in summer and fall.

SASSAFRAS ALBIDUM

SASS-a-frass al-BY-dum

Sassafras

Sassafras albidum

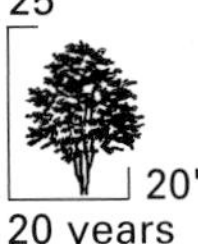

- **Pale yellow flowers as leaves unfurl, midspring**
- **Distinctive leaf color in autumn, some years**
- **Rich brown furrowed bark**
- **Zones 5 to 9**

This native of eastern North America grows 60 feet tall in time. It is sometimes disdained as a denizen of hedgerows and dry banks, but it can also be a beautiful shade tree with multiseasonal color. It branches like flowering dogwood, producing a horizontally layered look, and its flowering spans that of Eastern redbud *(Cercis canadensis)* and flowering dogwood *(Cornus florida)*. Its leaves are mitten-shaped, with one, two, or no lobes; in a good year they turn orange-red in autumn.
USES: Shade tree, or massed in a grove.
CULTURE: Transplanting dug plants is difficult; pot-grown plants transplant easily. Once established, sassafras will grow in almost any well-drained soil. It needs full sun or only light shade. If planted in a lawn space, mowing will remove most of the sucker shoots that appear around the plant. Those that remain can be snipped off.

SOPHORA JAPONICA

so-FOR-a (or SOPH-or-a) ja-PON-i-ka

Japanese pagoda tree

- Yellowish white flowers mid- to late summer
- Round-headed large tree
- Lustrous dark green foliage
- Zones 6 to 9, milder parts of Zone 5

This fine shade tree from China and Korea grows to 75 feet tall and nearly as wide. Its compound leaves, with leaflets nearly as small as those of honeylocust (*Gleditsia triacanthos*), provide filtered shade that allows turfgrass to grow well underneath. Its large masses of small flowers against the handsome foliage are striking in late summer, and the constricted bright green pods that follow keep the tree interesting through autumn.

USES: Shade tree for lawn or patio.

CULTURE: Does well in any well-drained soil, even slightly alkaline (to pH 7.5), with full sun. Tolerates dry soils and urban sites.

CULTIVARS: 'PNI 5625' (Regent™ scholar tree) is a superior selection. 'Princeton Upright' is more narrow than high. 'Pendula' is strongly weeping, useful for accent.

Sophora japonica

SORBUS ALNIFOLIA

SOR-bus al-ni-FOL-ee-a

Korean mountain ash

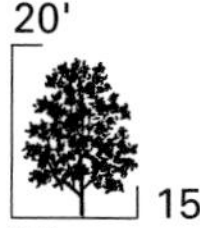

- White flowers, late spring
- Crisp dark green leaves turn golden orange in autumn
- Small red-orange fruits persist after leaf drop
- Silvery-gray twigs and branches
- Zones 5 to 7, milder parts of Zone 4

This mountain ash, from China, Japan, and Korea, grows 50 feet tall and wide, with simple leaves, unlike the compound leaves of other mountain ashes. It is colorful almost year-round.

USES: Lawn shade tree.

CULTURE: Prefers well-drained soils in full sun. Unlike most other mountain ashes, it is resistant to borers, but it is susceptible to fire blight in areas where that disease is prevalent.

CULTIVARS: 'Redbird' is a narrow variant, only half as wide as it is tall.

RELATED SPECIES: *S. americana* (American mountain ash), *S. aucuparia* (European mountain ash), and *S. decora* (showy mountain ash) are similar to one another and susceptible to borers, with less autumn foliage color than *S. alnifolia*.

Sorbus alnifolia

SPIRAEA JAPONICA

spy-REE-a ja-PON-i-ka

Japanese spirea

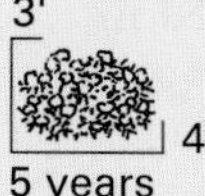

- Rose to white flowers early to midsummer
- Small deciduous shrub
- Foliage color varies
- Zones 4 to 8

This 2-foot shrub continues flowering intermittently after the first flush of color has passed. Summer and autumn foliage colors vary according to cultivar.

USES: Massed dooryard planting or in the front of a shrub border.

CULTURE: Grows well in any well-drained soil, even if dry. Flowers best in full sun but tolerates light shade.

CULTIVARS: 'Albiflora' has white flowers. 'Alpina' is an elegant dwarf with a refined habit and soft rose-pink flowers in early and midsummer. 'Anthony Waterer', the oldest selection, has dull rose-pink flowers. 'Coccinea', 'Dart's Red', and 'Neon Flash' have brighter rose-red flowers. 'Froebelii' is vigorous, growing to 3 feet tall. 'Goldmound' is compact, with bronze-red new foliage, turning and remaining golden yellow, with pink flowers early. 'Little Princess' is similar to 'Goldmound' in size, with pink flowers and fine-textured pale green foliage that turns deep red in autumn. 'Shibori' ('Shirobana') forms a loose mound and is distinctive for its multicolored flowers: pink, red, and white.

Spiraea japonica *'Gold Flame'*

SPIRAEA X VANHOUTTEI

spy-REE-a van-HOOT-ee-eye

Vanhoutte spirea

Spiraea × vanhouttei

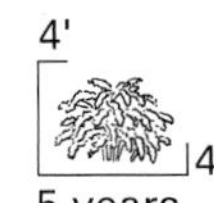

- White flowers, late spring, against blue-green foliage
- Graceful shrub to 5 feet tall
- Zones 4 to 8

This graceful hybrid of *S. cantoniensis* and *S. trilobata* has arching branches that are showy when covered with masses of white flowers.

USES: Specimen, in a shrub border, or massed.

CULTURE: Grows well in any well-drained soil, even though dry; best in full sun.

CULTIVAR: 'Renaissance' is resistant to leaf-spot diseases.

RELATED SPECIES: *S. cantoniensis* (Reeves spirea) is similar to Vanhoutte spirea but a little larger; it performs better in warm climates (Zones 7 to 9). *S. trilobata* (threelobe spirea), from central and northeastern Asia, is smaller and more cold-hardy. *S. nipponica* (Nippon spirea) 'Snowmound' is stiffly upright with outward-arching branches. It has white flowers and deep blue-green foliage. *S. prunifolia* (bridalwreath spirea), from eastern Asia, has gracefully arching branches, double white flowers in midspring, and handsome glossy leaves that turn orange-red in autumn.

STEWARTIA PSEUDOCAMELLIA

stew-ART-ee-a soo-doe-ca-MEAL-ya

Japanese stewartia

Stewartia pseudocamellia

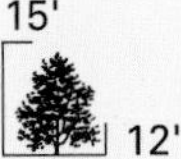

- Single camellialike white flowers, mid- to late summer
- Rich green leaves turn red-purple in autumn
- Molded trunks with multicolored bark
- Zones 6 to 8

This magnificent 35-foot tree is striking in the landscape at all seasons because of its molded trunk and branches, unexcelled bark interest, and 2-inch white flowers with golden centers.

USES: Specimen tree for lawn, border, or Japanese garden.

CULTURE: Needs well-drained, acidic soil (below pH 6.0) and some sun, but does best with partial shade in hot summers.

CULTIVAR: 'Ballet' has a gracefully arching habit and unusually large flowers, to 3½ inches across.

RELATED SPECIES: *S. monadelpha* (Hime-syara stewartia) grows to 50 feet, with smaller flowers and subtly bicolored cinnamon-brown bark. *S. pteropetiolata* var. *koreana* (Korean stewartia), once called *S. koreana* or *S. pseudocamellia* 'Korean Splendor', is native to Korea, with larger flowers, brighter autumn foliage, and equally showy bark. It is slightly more cold-hardy than the species.

STYRAX JAPONICUM

STY-rax ja-PON-i-cum

Japanese snowbell

Styrax japonicum

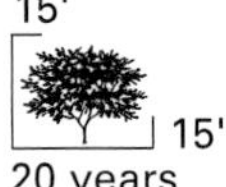

- White flowers, late spring
- Small tree with horizontal branching
- Smooth dark gray bark on sinewy branches
- Zones 7 and 8, milder parts of Zone 6

This small tree grows 25 to 30 feet tall and wider. Its bell-shaped flowers with spreading petals hang in pendulous clusters below the rich green foliage canopy.

USES: Plant this tree where it can be enjoyed by looking up into its flowering canopy, such as next to a patio.

CULTURE: Best in moist, well-drained soil in full sun to partial shade in the South, and away from strong winds.

CULTIVARS: 'Carillon' is semipendulous, with white flowers. 'Pink Chimes' is also semipendulous but with small clear pink flowers. 'Roseum' has pink flowers.

RELATED SPECIES: *S. americanum* (American snowbell) is similar but smaller, hardly more than a shrub, to 10 feet tall. *S. obassia* (fragrant snowbell) grows to about the same height as Japanese snowbell but is much more upright in habit, with large rounded leaves, to 10 inches across, and fragrant flowers in 4- to 8-inch pendulous clusters, very showy from beneath.

SYRINGA MEYERI 'PALIBIN'

sir-ING-ga MY-er-eye

'Palibin' Meyer lilac

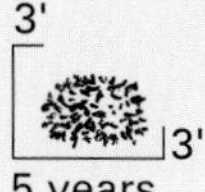

- Pale purple flowers, late spring
- Globose mound to 5 feet
- Lustrous rich green foliage
- Zones 4 to 7

This small shrub from northern China has good foliage, and its size makes it useful, but the main interest is in its colorful flowers.

USES: Specimen in a shrub border, massing, or entrance planting.

CULTURE: Needs well-drained soil and as much sun as possible. Is seldom bothered by mildew.

CULTIVAR: 'Palibin' may be the only form that is commercially available.

RELATED SPECIES: *S. microphylla* 'Superba', from China, is a loosely graceful shrub to 5 feet, with light green foliage and bright pink flowers in spring and again in late summer. *S. patula* (Korean lilac) 'Miss Kim' is a compact selection that starts out small but eventually reaches 8 feet in height and spread, remaining full at the base. It has dark green foliage and is useful as a screen. With its light purple flowers, it is in effect a larger version of 'Palibin'.

Syringa meyeri *'Palibin'*

SYRINGA X PRESTONIAE

sir-ING-ga press-TONE-ee-eye

Preston late lilacs

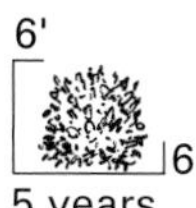

- White, pink, or purple flowers two weeks after common lilacs
- Large, fast-growing shrubs
- Zones 3 to 7, part of Zone 2 (extremely cold-hardy)

These vigorous and colorful hybrids of *S. villosa* (late lilac) and *S. reflexa* (nodding lilac), from northern China, are valued in the far north for their cold-hardiness.

USES: Specimens for flower color in early summer, after the common lilacs have finished; also in a shrub border or as a screen.

CULTURE: Needs well-drained soil and full sun for best flowering. Oystershell scale can occasionally be a problem.

CULTIVARS: At least a dozen are available. 'Agnes Smith' has white flowers. 'James MacFarlane' has quantities of pink flowers and lighter green foliage. 'Miss Canada' has the deepest pink flowers of all. 'Donald Wyman' and 'Nellie Bean' have deep purple flowers. 'Nocturne' has bluish-lilac flowers.

RELATED SPECIES AND HYBRIDS: *S. villosa* has a better moundlike form than its hybrids, with pale rosy-lilac to whitish flowers. Like the hybrids, it is not very fragrant.

Syringa × prestoniae *'Audrey'*

SYRINGA RETICULATA

sir-ING-ga ret-tic-yew-LAY-ta

Japanese tree lilac

15'
15'
20 years

- White flowers, early summer
- Small to medium tree
- Heart-shaped dark green leaves
- Zones 3 to 7

This small tree can eventually grow 25 to 30 feet tall. Its creamy white flowers open a month after those of common lilac, but many plants do not flower fully every year. Its leaves are similar to those of common lilac but larger, and its bark is vaguely cherrylike.

USES: Shade or patio tree, or in a shrub border.

CULTURE: Needs well-drained soil and full sun.

CULTIVARS AND VARIETIES: 'Ivory Silk' is a Canadian selection with upright, symmetrical form and good flowering as a young tree. 'Summer Snow' is rounded and compact, flowering heavily. The var. *mandschurica* (Manchurian tree lilac) is smaller and more shrubby, hardy to Zone 2.

RELATED SPECIES: *S. pekinensis* (Peking lilac), a shrubby tree from northern China, is about the same size as Japanese tree lilac, with similar flowering. Its exfoliating amber-brown bark is seen in the extreme in the selection 'Morton' (China Snow™).

Syringa reticulata

SYRINGA VULGARIS

sir-ING-ga vul-GARE-iss

Common lilac

Syringa vulgaris

Syringa vulgaris *'Mme Lemoine'*

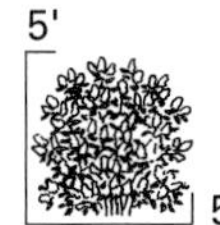

- **Fragrant, showy flowers in mid- to late spring**
- **Large, suckering shrub**
- **Dark green foliage**
- **Zones 4 to 7, part of Zone 3**

This long-cultivated shrub, native to southeastern Europe and widely naturalized elsewhere, has large clusters of wonderfully fragrant purple, magenta, lilac, pink, blue, white, and even pale yellow flowers, for which many people feel nostalgia. It has little other seasonal color.

USES: Background of a shrub border, or specimen for fragrance elsewhere.

CULTURE: Needs well-drained soil and full sun. Cutting off spent flower heads (deadheading) to curtail fruiting improves flower bud formation for the following year. Gradual renewal pruning of older plants is necessary; too much pruning at one time can reduce flowering for a year or two. Suckers may be removed, or thinned out and left to broaden the plant. In parts of Zones 5 to 7 with hot, humid summers, and in California, mildew can be a serious problem in late summer.

CULTIVARS: There are hundreds. Color, availability, size, and form should be considered in selection. A few of the most popular cultivars include 'Angel White' and 'Avalanche' (single white), 'Edith Cavell' (double white), 'President Grevy' (double blue), 'Michel Buchner' (double lilac), 'Katherine Havemeyer' (double lavender-pink), 'Andenken an Ludwig Spaeth' (single red-purple), 'Charles Joly' (double red-purple), 'Krasavitsa Moskvy' (pearly pink buds opening faint pink with a silvery tinge), and 'Sensation' (deep red-purple flowers with white petal margins).

RELATED SPECIES AND HYBRIDS: *S. oblata* var. *dilatata* (Korean early lilac) is similar to *S. vulgaris* but flowers a week earlier. It is cold-hardy in Zone 3 and parts of Zone 2 and is a parent of *S.* × *hyacinthiflora*. *S.* × *hyacinthiflora*, a hybrid of common lilac and Korean early lilac, includes outstanding and extremely hardy cultivars (to parts of Zone 2), including 'Asessippi' (single pale lavender), 'Maiden's Blush' (single true pink), 'Mount Baker' (single white), and 'Pocahontas' (single deep purple).

S. × *chinensis* (Chinese lilac) is a hybrid of common lilac and *S.* × *persica*, with smaller leaves and large clusters of faintly fragrant lavender to red-purple flowers that make it the showiest of lilacs. 'Alba' has white flowers; 'Saugeana' has bright reddish-violet flowers.

TAMARIX RAMOSISSIMA

TAM-a-rix ram-oh-SIS-sim-a

Five-stamen tamarisk

Tamarix ramosissima

- **Masses of small pink flowers in midsummer**
- **Shrub, 10 to 12 feet tall and wide, over time**
- **Fine texture, with tiny bright to bluish-green leaves**
- **Zones 4 to 9**

This airy shrub with arching branches, from southeastern Europe and central Asia, is colorful as it flowers in midsummer. Flowering continues at a lower intensity through late summer. The overall effect is a mist of rosy pink superimposed on a mist of green.

USES: Specimen in a shrub border or alone for accent.

CULTURE: Needs well-drained soil and full sun for best effect. Tolerates dryness, wind, and salt.

CULTIVAR: 'Summer Glow' is a superior selection with deep pink flowers and silvery blue-green foliage, vigorous and hardy.

RELATED SPECIES: *T. parviflora* (small-flowered tamarix), a native of southern Europe, bears soft pink flowers on old wood from buds formed the previous year. Because of this, it flowers in spring and should be pruned immediately after flowering, like forsythia. It is useful in Zones 5 to 9.

VIBURNUM SPECIES

vie-BUR-num

Viburnums

- Showy flowers and fruits
- Some have fragrant flowers
- Shrubs of all sizes and forms
- Some have colorful fall foliage
- Wide range of adaptation

Most of these shrubs are colorful or interesting in more than one season.

USES: Many are excellent neutral plants, good for background, filler, and a wide range of architectural uses.

CULTURE: Viburnums need well-drained soil and adequate moisture. Appropriate light conditions vary with species. Most are trouble-free. Borers are not likely to become serious if site needs are met.

SPECIES AND CULTIVARS:

***V. × burkwoodii* (Burkwood viburnum),** a *V. carlesii* hybrid, grows to 8 feet tall and wide, with small, lustrous dark green leaves that may turn yellowish to wine red before falling in early winter. Useful in Zones 6 to 8 and milder parts of Zone 5. 'Mohawk', a hybrid of *V. × burkwoodii* and *V. carlesii,* is hardy in Zone 5, with buds that are bright red for weeks before they open white.

V. × burkwoodii

***V. × carlcephalum* (fragrant snowball),** taller than its parent, *V. carlesii,* has larger flower clusters and is hardy in Zones 5 to 8.

V. × carlcephalum

***V. carlesii* (Korean spice viburnum),** a Korean native, usually remains below 6 feet, with velvety to sandpapery rounded leaves that may turn reddish in autumn. Its white flowers, pink in bud, have a delightful clove fragrance, present in its hybrids. Its fruits are reddish in autumn, but do not always form. Zones 5 to 7 and milder parts of Zone 4. 'Compactum' is usually less than 4 to 5 feet tall.

V. carlesii

***V. davidii* (David viburnum),** from China, is one of the more attractive evergreen viburnums, growing 3 feet high and wider, with elegant foliage. Its dark blue fruits show to good effect against the dark green leaves. Useful in Zones 8 and 9 and milder parts of Zone 7.

V. davidii

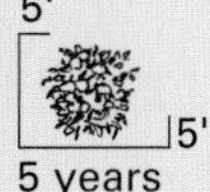

***V. dentatum* (arrowwood viburnum),** a native shrub of eastern North America, has toothed leaves and clusters of white flowers in late spring. Blue-black fruits add interest after leaf drop. Useful in Zones 4 to 9, if seeds from nearby sources are used. 'Synnestvedt' (Emerald Lustre™) has outstanding lustrous foliage.

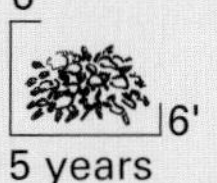

***V. dilatatum* (linden viburnum)** is one of the best for seasonal interest, with large clusters of creamy white flowers in late spring, followed by showy clusters of bright red berries, which remain colorful until December, sometimes longer. It grows 5 to 8 feet tall, depending on the cultivar. 'Catskill' grows only 5 feet tall and half again as wide, with showy flowers and fruits and excellent dark green foliage.

V. dilatatum

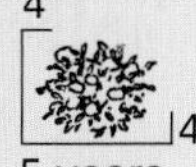

***V. × juddii* (Judd viburnum),** a hybrid of *V. carlesii,* grows to 8 feet tall and wide. It is more open than *V. carlesii* and fully as hardy.

V. lantana *'Mohican'*

7' 6' 5 years

***V. lantana* (wayfaring tree),** a large European shrub, has deciduous, roundish dark green leaves, fuzzy underneath. Its white flowers are much like those of *V. dentatum* or *V. prunifolium,* but its fruits pass through several color changes: greenish yellow, orange, and red, finally ripening black. It is more drought-tolerant than most viburnums, and useful in Zones 4 to 7. 'Mohican' holds its fruits in the orange stage for nearly a month before they ripen black.

7' 6' 5 years

***V. odoratissimum* (sweet viburnum)** grows 12 to 15 feet tall and wide, making a large mass of evergreen foliage. Its fragrant white flowers, in 4-inch clusters, open in midspring, and the fruits that follow turn red, then ripen black. It is useful in Zones 9 and 10. 'Awabuki', also called the leatherleaf form of *V. odoratissimum* in the southeastern states, grows to the same size, with stiff, glossy leaves to 6 inches long. It is hardier, at least to Zone 8.

6' 6' 5 years

***V. opulus* (European cranberrybush)** grows to 10 feet tall, making an effective screen. Its white flowers, in flat clusters, open in late spring, and its red fruits are showy from late summer to midwinter, sometimes longer. 'Roseum' (European snowball) has all-sterile snowball-type flowers, so it produces no fruit, and is often badly disfigured by aphids. 'Compactum'

V. opulus *'Roseum'*

grows to only 6 feet tall but is otherwise like the species. Useful in Zones 4 to 8 and milder parts of Zone 3.

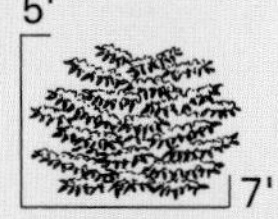

V. plicatum, from Asia, comes in two forms. F. *plicatum* (Japanese snowball) has all-sterile snowball flowers. It lacks fruiting interest and is hardy only in Zones 6 to 8. The other form, f. *tomentosum* (double-file viburnum), has small fertile

V. plicatum *'Lanarth'*

flowers in flat clusters, ringed with showy sterile florets, for a lace-doily effect. The fertile flowers develop into small red fruit in late summer, and the foliage turns reddish in autumn. The fertile form is also hardier, in much of Zone 5. Because of its horizontal branching, accentuated by the flowers and fruits, it is one of the most sought-after flowering shrubs. 'Mariesii' and 'Shasta' are superb and 'Shoshoni' is similar but grows to only 4 feet tall and twice as wide.

***V. prunifolium* (black haw),** a stiffly upright shrub, native to eastern North America, grows 12 to 15 feet tall and nearly as wide in Zones 4 to 8 and milder parts of Zone 3. It has clusters of white flowers, smooth leaves that turn reddish in autumn, and fruits that turn from yellow-green to reddish, then ripen blue-black. It can be trained as a small tree.

V. prunifolium

***V. × rhytidophylloides* (lantanaphyllum viburnum),** a hybrid of *V. lantana* and the evergreen leatherleaf viburnum, is semievergreen, with longer and more wrinkled leaves than *V. lantana.* It is a good screen, growing 8 feet tall and nearly as wide. It flowers in midspring and, in some cultivars, again in late summer. Useful in Zones 6 to 8. 'Willow Wood' flowers heavily in fall and again in spring.

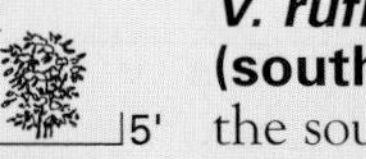

***V. rufidulum* (southern black haw),** the southern counterpart of *V. prunifolium,* is similar in size, function, flowering and fruiting but has glossy, leathery leaves that turn purple-red to brilliant scarlet in autumn. It is useful in Zones 5 to 9, if seed from nearby sources is used.

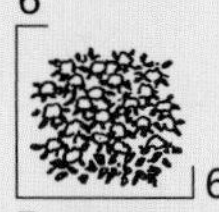

***V. trilobum* (American cranberrybush)** is almost identical to *V. opulus* except that it has good reddish autumn foliage and is hardier, to all of Zone 3.

V. trilobum

VITEX AGNUS-CASTUS

VYE-tex AG-nus CAST-us

Chaste tree

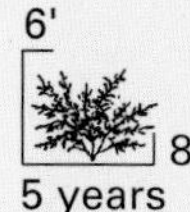

- **Pale violet flowers, late summer**
- **Cut-back shrub to small tree**
- **Aromatic foliage**
- **Zones 6 to 10+**

This shrub from southern Europe has late-summer flowers in light purple, pink, blue, or white. In Zones 9 to 10+, it makes a large shrub or multiple-trunked tree, growing to 15 feet tall and wide; in Zones 7 and 8, it is smaller, depending on winter climate; in Zone 6 it is best used as a cut-back shrub, growing 4 to 5 feet tall each summer.

USES: Specimen or shrub border, for color.

CULTURE: Best in well-drained soil and full sun. Tolerates heat and dryness but does better with moderate water.

CULTIVARS: 'Alba' and 'Silver Spire' (white), 'Abbeville Blue' and 'Colonial Blue' (blue), 'Blushing Spires' and 'Rosea' (pink), 'Fletcher Pink' (lavender-pink), and others.

RELATED SPECIES: *V. incisa* (cut-leaved chaste tree) from southern Asia has finely cut silvery-green foliage and lilac to lavender flowers. Similar to chaste tree except hardy to Zone 6.

Vitex agnus-castus

WEIGELA FLORIDA

wye-JEEL-a FLOR-i-da

Old-fashioned weigela

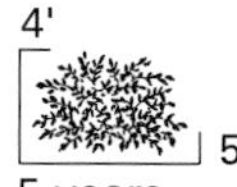

- **Showy flowers, late spring**
- **No autumn color**
- **Some newer cultivars have colorful foliage in summer**
- **Zones 5 to 9, depending on cultivar**

Some of the newer cultivars of this old-fashioned plant bear showy flowers and brightly colored foliage. The species has little to recommend it beyond its brief spring display.

USES: Shrub border, specimen for accent, or mass plantings.

CULTURE: Best in well-drained soil with adequate moisture, in full sun to half shade. The most vigorous types need annual pruning, after flowering.

CULTIVARS: 'Red Prince' is the best red-flowered form, hardy at least to milder parts of Zone 4. 'Minuet' has purple-tinted leaves and purplish-red flowers, and is hardy to milder parts of Zone 3. 'Alexandra' (Wine and Roses™) has deep purple foliage and rosy-pink flowers. 'French Lace' has red flowers and yellow leaf margins. 'Rubidor' has bright yellow leaves and ruby-red flowers. 'Variegata' is an older selection with creamy pale yellow-variegated leaves and light pink flowers.

Weigela florida *'Rubidor'*

YUCCA FILAMENTOSA

YUK-ka fill-a-men-TOE-sa

Adam's needle

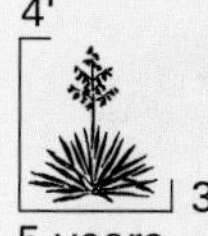

- **Creamy white flowers, early summer**
- **Thick 3-foot evergreen leaves**
- **Zones 5 to 10**

This clump of swordlike blue-green leaves grows 2 feet tall; stalks bearing 3-inch flowers rise to 5 feet in early summer.

USES: Mass planting, or specimen for accent.

CULTURE: Needs well-drained soil and full sun. Tolerates very dry soils. Leaf tips are sharp; not appropriate in spots where children play.

CULTIVARS: 'Bright Edge' and 'Gold Edge' have deep blue-green leaves with broad yellow edges. 'Color Guard' has ivory yellow stripes. 'Golden Sword' has yellow stripes down the leaf centers. 'Ivory Tower' is robust, with large branched flower stalks, to 6 feet.

RELATED SPECIES: *Y. glauca* (soapweed), native from South Dakota to New Mexico, has strongly bluish leaves the same length as those of Adam's needle but much narrower. It is useful as a specimen for accent, or in small groupings, in Zones 4 to 7.

Yucca filamentosa

Mail-order Sources of Flowering Trees and Shrubs

Arborvillage
P.O. Box 227
Holt, MO 64048
816-264-3911
email: arborvillage@aol.com
Trees and shrubs

Bovees Nursery
1737 SW Coronado
Portland, OR 97219
800-435-9250
www.bovees.com
Rhododendrons and azaleas

Camellia Forest Nursery
9701 Carrie Road
Chapel Hill, NC 27516
919-968-0504
www.camforest.com
Camellias and other trees and shrubs

Carroll Gardens
444 E. Main Street
Westminster, MD 21157
800-638-6334
www.carrollgardens.com
Perennials, trees, and shrubs

Eastern Plant Specialties
Box 226
Georgetown, ME 04548
732-382-2508
www.easternplant.com
Trees, shrubs, and perennials

Forestfarm
990 Tetherow Road
Williams, OR 97544
541-846-7269
www.forestfarm.com
Large list, including rare plants

Gossler Farms Nursery
1200 Weaver Road
Springfield, OR 97478
541-746-3922
Magnolias and other trees and shrubs

Greer Gardens
1280 Goodpasture Island Road
Eugene, OR 97401
800-548-0111
www.greergardens.com
Rhododendrons and other trees and shrubs

Heirloom Roses
24062 NE Riverside Drive
St. Paul, OR 97137
503-538-1576
www.heirloomroses.com
Old garden roses

Louisiana Nursery
5853 Highway 182
Opelousas, LA 70570
337-948-3696
www.Durionursery.com
Large list of trees and shrtubs for the South

Mellinger's
2310 W South Range Road
North Lima, OH 44452-9731
800-321-7444
www.mellingers.com
Wide variety of plants

Roses of Yesterday & Today
803 Brown's Valley Road
Watsonville, CA 95076
831-728-1901
www.rosesofyesterday.com
Wide selection of roses

Roslyn Nursery
211 Burr's Lane
Dix Hills, NY 11746
631-643-9347
www.roslynnursery.com
Large list of trees, shrubs, and perennials

Siskiyou Rare Plant Nursery
2825 Cummings Road
Medford, OR 97501
541-772-6846
Large list of small shrubs and perennials

Wayside Gardens
1 Garden Lane
Hodges, SC 29695
800-845-1124
www.waysidegardens.com
Trees, shrubs, and perennials

White Flower Farm
P.O. Box 50
Litchfield, CT 06759-0050
800-503-9624
www.whiteflowerfarm.com
Shrubs and perennials

Woodlanders Inc.
1128 Colleton Avenue
Aiken, SC 29801
803-648-7522
www.woodlanders.net
Native trees, shrubs, and perennials

Yucca Do Nursery
P.O. Box 907
Hempstead, TX 77445
979-826-4580
www.yuccado.com
Rare and unusual plants for the Southwest

Many mail-order nurseries specialize in certain groups of plants that can be hard to find, such as unusual rhododendrons and azaleas, magnolias, miniature plants, and regional native plants.

USDA Plant Hardiness Zone Map

This map of climate zones helps you select plants for your garden that will survive a typical winter in your region. The United States Department of Agriculture (USDA) developed the map, basing the zones on the lowest recorded temperatures across North America. Zone 1 is the coldest area and Zone 11 is the warmest.

Plants are classified by the coldest temperature and zone they can endure. For example, plants hardy to Zone 6 survive where winter temperatures drop to –10° F. Those hardy to Zone 8 die long before it's that cold. These plants may grow in colder regions but must be replaced each year. Plants rated for a range of hardiness zones can usually survive winter in the coldest region as well as tolerate the summer heat of the warmest one.

To find your hardiness zone, note the approximate location of your community on the map, then match the color band marking that area to the key.

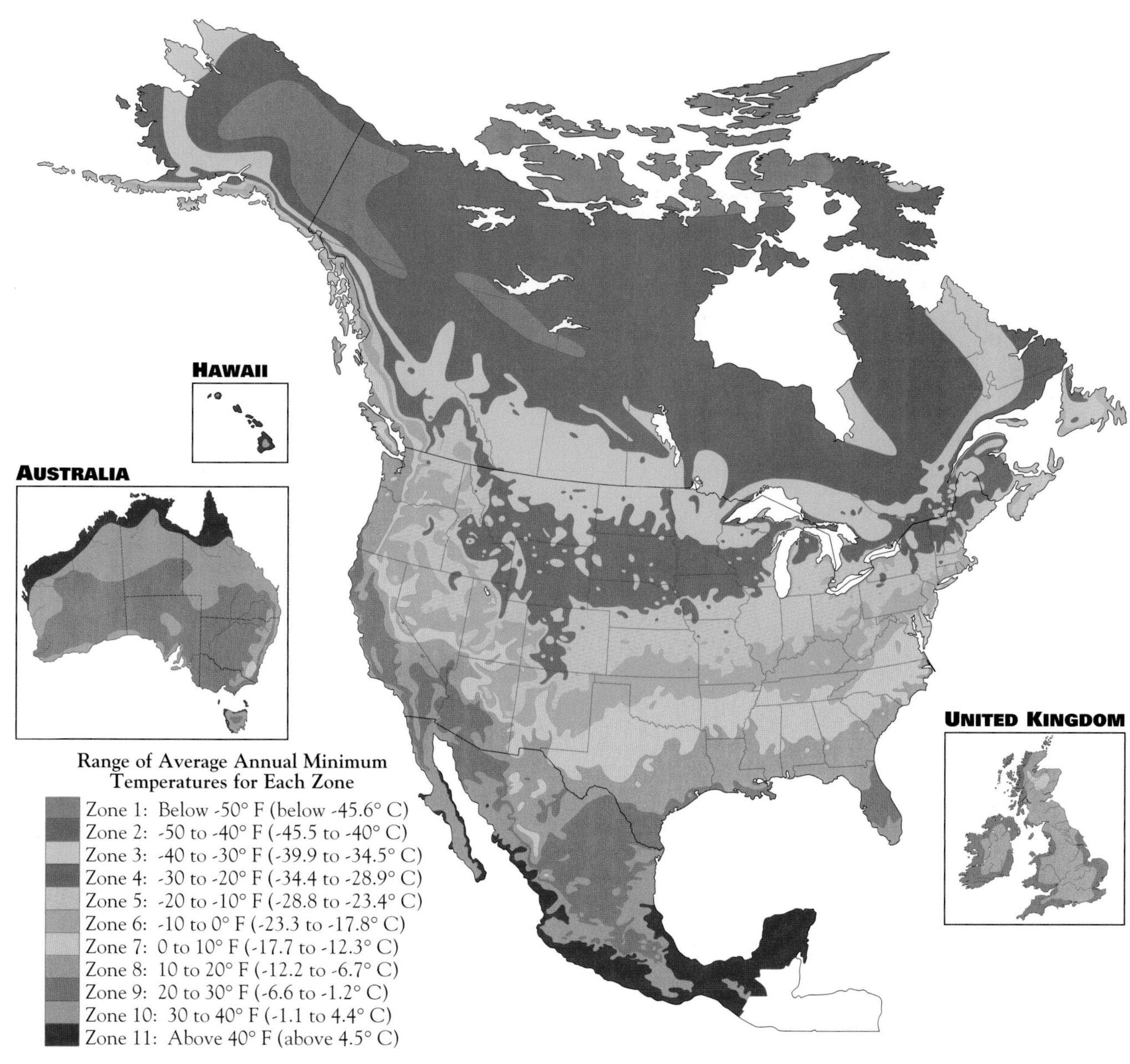

INDEX

Page references in **bold type** indicate Gallery or Problem Solver entries and always contain a photograph. Page references in *italic type* indicate other photographs.

Metric Conversions

U.S. Units to Metric Equivalents			**Metric Units to U.S. Equivalents**		
To Convert From	Multiply By	To Get	To Convert From	Multiply By	To Get
Inches	25.4	Millimeters	Millimeters	0.0394	Inches
Inches	2.54	Centimeters	Centimeters	0.3937	Inches
Feet	30.48	Centimeters	Centimeters	0.0328	Feet
Feet	0.3048	Meters	Meters	3.2808	Feet
Yards	0.9144	Meters	Meters	1.0936	Yards
Square inches	6.4516	Square centimeters	Square centimeters	0.1550	Square inches
Square feet	0.0929	Square meters	Square meters	10.764	Square feet
Square yards	0.8361	Square meters	Square meters	1.1960	Square yards
Acres	0.4047	Hectares	Hectares	2.4711	Acres
Cubic inches	16.387	Cubic centimeters	Cubic centimeters	0.0610	Cubic inches
Cubic feet	0.0283	Cubic meters	Cubic meters	35.315	Cubic feet
Cubic feet	28.316	Liters	Liters	0.0353	Cubic feet
Cubic yards	0.7646	Cubic meters	Cubic meters	1.308	Cubic yards
Cubic yards	764.55	Liters	Liters	0.0013	Cubic yards

To convert from degrees Fahrenheit (F) to degrees Celsius (C), first subtract 32, then multiply by 5/9.

To convert from degrees Celsius to degrees Fahrenheit, multiply by 9/5, then add 32.